P9-AFD-799

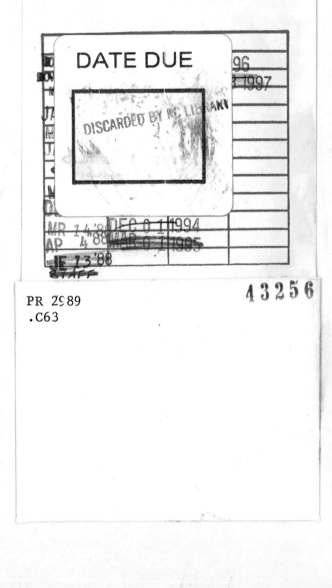

SHAKESPEARE'S
FOUR GIANTS

SHAKESPEARE'S FOUR GIANTS

By

BLANCHE COLES

RICHARD R. SMITH PUBLISHER, INC.

Rindge, New Hampshire

1957

Set up, printed and bound in
the United States of America by
The Colonial Press Inc.

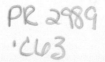

To

EDNA COX

who has been indefatigable and
discerning in seeing this manu-
script along the production path

CONTENTS

SHAKESPEARE'S
FOUR GIANTS

INTRODUCTION

SHAKESPEARE PORTRAYED many characters who were of near or full heroic stature. Even some of his secondary characters are of heroic mould. It was long believed, and taught, that Shakespeare followed the example of the ancient dramatists in presenting the great protagonists of his plays as having a fatal character flaw which in the end brought about their downfall. This interpretation is now being challenged. The fatal flaw is sometimes difficult to find in Shakespeare's heroes. The most gigantic of the long pageant of heroic characters are the protagonists of the four plays accounted the greatest: Hamlet, Macbeth, Othello, and King Lear.

In planning these brief character sketches of Shakespeare's four giants, I have been aware that it is impossible to disentangle one character completely from a play for the purpose of presenting a sketch of that one individual. However, an attempt can be made to concentrate on one character, disregarding, as much as possible, any careful study of other people in the play except where their actions have an important bearing on the main character, or protagonist, being studied. Some problems of the play may also be disregarded. For example, my study of the character of Hamlet is not a complete study of the play by that name, and my study of Macbeth is a study only of Macbeth the man, not a study of the entire play. Any reader who takes up this book with the expectation of finding the old problems haggled over will be keenly disappointed. Also, one must note that any study of *Othello* becomes largely a study of Iago.

On the whole my interpretations differ quite widely from the commonly accepted ones, especially those that have found such favor that one would scarcely dare to dispute them, such as the almost ineradicable view that Hamlet was a procrastinator. If I did not feel reasonably certain of having some new and worth while viewpoints to offer, I would not attempt to add another volume to this book-cluttered world. However, I must not begin by telling you that Hamlet was not a procrastinator, that Macbeth was not a murderer, that Iago was not jealous of Cassio because of the promotion or that Lear was not foolish almost to insanity in dividing his kingdom. But hear me through, and I may be able to convince at least some of you that there has been much muddy thinking about Shakespeare and much innocent misrepresentation even by scholarly people. Many of these scholarly people are teachers whose full schedules do not permit them to sit by the hour thinking and thinking of the play they are studying. Perhaps part of the fault lies in the fact that one commentator may have put his theory so convincingly that others follow like sheep, though they do not think of themselves as sheep. So thoroughly are they convinced of the other man's wisdom that they accept his word and fail to think the thing through for themselves, even omitting to look up the meaning of possible obsolete words, only one of which might change the entire significance of a passage.

One satisfactory approach to the study of a single character is to read only the lines of that person throughout the play, omitting all other lines except as memory connects them with the speech of the character under consideration. This separating of a person's lines often proves to be very revealing even in the study of minor characters. Such a procedure, of course, presupposes an adequate knowledge of the drama being studied. This plan has been pursued largely in the four sketches here presented.

The style adopted in this book differs from that used in my *Shakespeare Studies*, where I kept a strictly objective viewpoint. In this book, I shall reserve the privilege of saying "you" and "I" and "he," the "he" usually being a writer with whom I may or may not agree. It will be necessary to follow the story to some extent, but for the most part the reader's familiarity with the play will be taken for granted.

My sketch of Hamlet is the shortest of the group. So very much has been written about Hamlet, much of it altogether worthless today, that about all that can be accomplished in a brief character sketch, such as I have attempted, is to create an atmosphere, try to trace Hamlet's thought throughout the play and add a few new viewpoints one may have glimpsed through many readings of the play.

Being a "Bradleyite" with some little reservations that may be presumptuous, I think of Shakespeare's characters as real people. (The so-called "closet student" of Shakespeare endeavors to analyze the imagined real people with whom Shakespeare must have lived in the quiet of his study, weighing their actions and thoughts, while he was creating their counterparts to be presented on the stage.) This approach has made it seem reasonable for me to write in imaginary scenes and conversations that are not in the plays themselves. For this procedure, I have the authority of the eminent critic, Allardyce Nicoll,[1] who points out that Shakespeare himself has given us clues for the imaginative creation of conversations and actions not actually put upon the stage. I have availed myself of this Shakespeare-granted privilege in all four of my sketches.

This book has not been written for the use of any particular class or group of students but is presented for the consideration of Shakespeare lovers anywhere.

[1] *Shakespeare*, An *Introduction to his works*.

HAMLET

HAMLET

WITTENBERG WAS not a co-educational institution. It is possible, even probable, that Hamlet, taking heavy courses in philosophy and doing post-graduate work, had little time for social life and that girls and women played a small part in his little world. His thoughts and ideas of the fair sex, then, centered around his still beautiful mother and the little Ophelia whom he had seen around the court at Kronberg, growing into a lovely, flower-like creature who had completely captivated his heart. Many times in his cloister-like rooms, at Wittenberg, when the hour had grown late he had put aside his books and had written long letters in which he poured out his love for Ophelia. These were precious, tranquil hours never to be forgotten. (Obviously the letters were not written after his return to Elsinore.)

Inextricably woven with his thoughts of his mother were pleasant pictures of his noble, handsome father and of his two parents together. They were a devoted, loving pair, a joy to their son as he grew to manhood and began, himself, to think seriously of the marriage state.

Then suddenly, without warning, there came into the peaceful quiet of those monastic-like rooms a messenger with the news of his father's sudden death.

In the presence of Death many things take on a shoddy look. Words that ordinarily carry their own dignity become cheap things. Commonplace words become pitifully paltry. To say that the news was a stunning blow makes the discussion of a great play sound like a description of a prize-fight on

TV, and yet it was just that. Hamlet was stunned as by a terrific blow, in the serious sense of these words it was a "stunning blow." He was shocked and bewildered. His first thought was of his own personal loss. Suddenly he realized that in all his life he never had met a serious situation without his father. Now in this most momentous crisis he felt inexpressibly helpless and alone. A great supporting strength had been removed.

For a long time he sat thinking, thinking about the noble man who had been his father. Occasionally he grasped the realization that his father was dead. It all seemed so impossible that he found himself resenting the thought, pushing it out of his mind, resenting the messenger who had brought the news. Then finally that awful, undeniable fact stood before him.

His own father was dead!

The silence of the room was broken by the opening of the door as his friend, Horatio, came in quietly to ask why he had not appeared in the dining hall. On being told the news Horatio sat with his friend for awhile, then began taking care of the practical arrangements for the journey home. As he supervised the packing and consulted about transportation, Horatio made a decision of his own. Since his sensitive fellow-student was so much in need of friendship he, Horatio, would follow and be with Hamlet after the first few days, or weeks, of bereavement spent with his mother.

On the journey home Hamlet's thoughts turned to his mother with a feeling of guilt that he had given so much consideration to his own loss. She would be prostrated with grief, and so he must put aside, as much as possible, his own personal sorrow and try to comfort and sustain his mother. He saw long years of lonely widowhood stretching before her, but found some consolation in the thought that he and Ophelia could do much to alleviate that loneliness.

The funeral had been postponed until Hamlet's arrival. As

he walked with his mother behind the body of his father, she leaned on him as she had been wont to lean upon his father. It pained him intensely to feel her body shaken with grief and to see her tears flowing so freely and unrestrained. He found himself thinking of Niobe.

But in a short time Hamlet's sensitiveness and his prophetic soul told him that all was not as he had pictured the home scene in his first hours of deepest sorrow. His mother was unbecomingly gay at times. She laughed and spent a great deal of time in the company of his uncle Claudius, his father's brother who bore no resemblance to Hamlet's father either in appearance or in character. Claudius was proclaimed King, and soon after he and Hamlet's mother were married—less than a month after King Hamlet's death, in fact. A grave disillusionment is beginning to settle down upon Hamlet.

Words cannot describe a serious disillusionment. Only an inadequate attempt can be made to suggest its benumbing of the senses, its blasting blow at all reasonable hope. The victim invariably walks with his head down. He loses interest in the lighter side of life in all its aspects. No form of amusement or entertainment can gain his attention. The most urgent responsibility is nothing to him. His mind goes 'round and 'round over the condition that caused the disillusionment. He sees no way out of his plight. No persuasion, no argument, no attempt at diversion can change his mental attitude or condition. He is alone—as much alone as if the earth had no other inhabitant. Such human contacts as he is obliged to meet leave no impression on him.

Our first view of Hamlet is at a meeting of the court in a room of the castle. Claudius, in a very elaborate, high-sounding speech, makes a public announcement of his marriage to his brother's widow. At the close of that part of his speech he reminds the lords that they have given their consent to the marriage, and he thanks them. There is a little business transacted, the familiar conversation between Hamlet and his mother takes place, and Hamlet promises not to return to Wittenberg. The King is well pleased with Hamlet's promise, his reason for making the request being that he wishes to have Hamlet where he can watch him. It does not matter to Hamlet whether he remains in Denmark or returns to Wittenberg.

The colorful retinue goes out leaving behind them mingled scents of vulgar perfumes. We can picture the Queen wearing a rich brocade cut in youthful lines and resplendent with jewels. The King has chosen for the occasion a luxurious velvet that becomes his still slender figure. The ladies wear colorful gowns of shimmering, swishing silk and the gentlemen their velvets that run from gay tones to shades of somber richness.

When the room is cleared of its glittering assemblage, a lone figure clad in black stands like the personification of desolation near the center of the room. Hamlet begins to speak.

Watch now! Remember that all Hamlet knows up to this time is that his father has been taken by death very suddenly and that his mother has made a hasty marriage. He knows nothing of the Ghost or its revelations. Yet he begins by wishing his too, too solid flesh would melt and that the Everlasting had not made a law against self-slaughter. Vehemently he exclaims to God and says the world in all its meaningless routine has come to seem weary, stale, flat and unprofitable to him. It has become like an unweeded garden where only things rank and gross are growing. Then the Prince begins to speak of his mother and her over-hasty marriage. His father had been dead less than a month—he was such an excellent King that was to the present King Hyperion to a satyr. He was so loving to Hamlet's mother, and she would hang on him as if she gained increasing strength from his love. Yet within a month—but he must not let himself think of it—suddenly he comes out with a generalization about all women when he says, "Frailty, thy name is woman." This probably is the most important line in the play. It tells (in five words) of his loss of faith in all womankind, and of his lonely disillusionment. But this line, as is the case with many other serious statements of Shakespeare, has been bandied about humorously until it has lost its original meaning to the average reader who has only heard it tittered about. Hamlet goes on to say that before the shoes she wore to his father's funeral were old she—but he cannot finish the sentence. His voice has begun to break, and now he buries his face in his hands so that his voice is muffled as he cries, God, God, a beast that is without the power of reason would have mourned longer! She was married to his uncle, he goes on, his father's brother but no more like his father than he to Hercules. Within a month—his words come chokingly now and his sentences are unfinished. Before the evidence of her weeping at his father's funeral had left her reddened eyes she married. Then the deepest pain of Hamlet's hurt comes out as he all but rails at the thought of his mother and his uncle hastening with such dispatch to incestuous sheets.

This then, stated plainly by Shakespeare in the early part of the play, is the cause of Hamlet's melancholia—the incestuous marriage of his mother and his uncle. A little later he will learn of their treachery to his father, and that will be the blow that fells him to his knees. This speech must be nailed down in memory and kept in mind until the end of the play. Throughout the reading we shall find that the very thought of his mother in his uncle's lustful embrace is hideous, revolting torture to him. And we find ourselves wanting to say with Hamlet, O God, a beast that lacks the power of reason would have mourned longer!

But this loathing of his mother's marriage does not remotely resemble the Oedipus complex that some recent scholars have suggested. Hamlet is not jealous of Claudius. He despises Claudius for what he is—a "bloody, bawdy villain, a remorseless, treacherous, lecherous, kindless villain."

Some of the critics have pointed out that Claudius is intelligent. Perhaps that should be granted to some extent. At least
he was clever enough to get himself elected before Hamlet
could make his claim to the crown. But the director who
gives the part of Claudius to a handsome matinee-idol type,
who could easily be mistaken for the hero of the play, and
then adds insult to injury by presenting a Hamlet who daw-
dles suggestively, almost indecently, over his mother has
much to learn about Shakespeare. Claudius was ill-favored
in appearance. Hamlet says it again and again. He says it to
his mother, and she does not deny it.

Just when Horatio arrived in Elsinore is not certain, but it
is most likely that it was after the funeral of King Hamlet.
At that time he would find his friend in deeper despair than
at their last meeting and, looking about him, it would not be
difficult to discover the cause of Hamlet's dark mood. Gertrude's infatuation for Claudius must have been obvious to
everyone in the Court, and the observant Horatio would not
fail to grasp the situation and to understand something of the
stress under which his friend was laboring. He would not in-
trude on such a delicate state of affairs, and so he remained
aloof from Hamlet, awaiting an opportunity to be of service
to him if that became possible.

Thus he spent a good deal of time on the ramparts. It was
an interesting place to loiter and a reasonably safe place to
hide. There he made the acquaintance of the guards. Often he
heard the old clock in the tower boom out the midnight hour.
Then the guard would change, and he would have a different
group to help him wile away the time. So he came to know
them all—Francisco, Bernardo, Marcellus, and possibly others. Also, they came to know and to trust him. It was through
these friendships that Hamlet came to the platform where
the King's ghost had made his mighty appearance. When the
Ghost appears and beckons Hamlet to a more remote ground,

Hamlet decides to go in spite of the importuning of his friends. So he goes bravely into the unknown.

Somehow our hearts go out to Hamlet more than to any of the other great giants, more than to the suffering Macbeth, more than to the tortured Othello, more than to the bewildered Lear. Hamlet is so young, so sensitively unprepared for the fate that is in store for him. We see him entering young manhood entertaining simple, wholesome dreams— dreams of his return to Elsinore when his studies were over, of his marriage to Ophelia, of a closer, growing companionship with his father, of a certain enjoyment of the court life presided over by his queenly mother, of sharing his father's duties more and more until that still far off time when the responsibilities of state would fall upon his own shoulders. Then suddenly, without warning Fate begins to rain blow after blow upon him until she has lashed him to his knees. The final blow comes when from his own father's lips he learns that his mother was unfaithful to him while he lived.

When Hamlet emerges from the conversation with his father's ghost he has a task laid upon him, a task which he has sworn solemnly to perform, a task which we know he does not perform. Scholars from Shakespeare's time to our own have asked "Why?" Why does he not go directly about the business and get it done?

There have been many answers to this question, many theories have been set forth with more or less convincing eloquence. Some of these have held the minds of students for a generation only to be discarded by the succeeding generation. One of the most tenacious of these theories was that of the sentimental Hamlet, built largely about Goethe's description of a "lovely pure and most moral nature without the strength of nerve that forms a hero, who sinks beneath a burden which it cannot bear and must not cast away." Then there was the Coleridgean theory of the tragedy of reflection which gave us a picture of a youth so much given to reflection and speculation that he became irresolute. This was the procrastinating Hamlet, still accepted by students who have put their books aside with their diplomas. There were other theories, and the overall result of pondering them left the average student with an indefinite, hazy picture of a weak-willed, weak-kneed, procrastinating creature whom Shakespeare never in the world would have considered as material for the protagonist of a play. There was another very alluring viewpoint, hardly a theory, proposed by William Hazlitt who said, in brief, "It is we who are Hamlet. . . . Whoever has become thoughtful and melancholy through his own mishaps or those of others; whoever has borne about with him the clouded brow of reflection . . . he who has felt his mind sink within him and sadness cling to his heart like a malady; whose powers of action have been eaten up by thought . . . whose bitterness of soul makes him careless of consequences . . . —this is the true Hamlet." This conception we once hugged to our breasts—before we had met a problem that could not be solved on a schoolroom desk—and we went mooning about, thinking of ourselves as a second Hamlet.

It was A. C. Bradley who cleared the atmosphere, as it were, and introduced us to the disillusioned Hamlet, and told us that Hamlet is enveloped in a dull apathetic gloom in which so far as analyzing his "duty" he is not thinking of it at all, but for the time literally forgets it.

Today, perhaps with a clearer understanding of modern psychology, such men as Joseph Quincy Adams tell us that Hamlet's condition was a complete paralysis of the will power which is inevitably linked with a deep melancholia. Hamlet's melancholy was induced in the first place by his father's sudden death which was followed by the (to him) heart-rending precipitation of his mother's marriage to his uncle. This is the condition in which we find him at the opening of the play—a brooding sadness envelops him. Then after the meeting with his father's Ghost the complete paralysis of the will and the complete melancholia settle down upon him. For along with the knowledge of his mother's unfaithfulness to his father comes the suspicion that she had a part in the murder of her husband. (The Ghost had not covered this point.) Also, lurking in the recesses of his troubled mind was the thought that Claudius was capable of seducing Ophelia, and he began thinking that the only safe place for her was a nunnery.

This, then, is the Hamlet that we must accept today, until a more convincing theory can be presented, a Hamlet whose will power is paralyzed as a result of a deep melancholia.

It is the Ghost who has called his brother an incestuous, adulterous beast, and the student who has become well enough acquainted with Shakespeare's methods of working will doubtless agree, without question, to the supposition that Shakespeare expects the Ghost's estimate of Claudius to be accepted.

Hamlet speaks of the smile of Claudius, an almost continuous smile. Even in a character-sketch of Hamlet that smile must be considered, because of its effect on Hamlet. There is a description of another man's smile that comes to the mind of a reading person—the smile of Nathaniel Hawthorne's Judge Pyncheon. Judge Pyncheon's smile was warm and sultry, radiating kindness which shone like a noonday sun along the streets or glowed like a household fire in the drawing rooms of his private acquaintances. One does not, I surmise, think of Claudius as having such a sunny, sultry smile. Rather was it not a more clever, ingratiating smile that purported to let the other person into his confidence and succeeded in spite of a shrewd, hard glitter in the eyes that should have warned any observant person? Perhaps Hamlet's prophetic soul had sensed that glitter.

The blow that Hamlet receives at the meeting with his father's Ghost is physical as well as mental. He is scarcely able to stand. Somehow he regains a certain control of himself and manages some conversation with his friends, extracting a promise from them not to reveal anything they have seen. And all the while in his own mind he is thinking that the time is out of joint, and he curses the malice of Fate that has sent him into the world to make the adjustments that the times require. This reflection should not be passed by lightly or ignored. The corrupt state of Denmark is almost as disturbing to him as his mother's defection.

After the meeting with the Ghost Hamlet is very close to a mental collapse. His mind goes 'round and 'round its dreary cycle—the knowledge of his mother's unfaithfulness to his father and the still more distracting suspicion of her as a murderess, until he is unable to concentrate on the admonition of the Ghost. There is, perhaps, no greater mental suffering than one in which the mind moves in a fixed groove of torment from which it cannot extricate itself. Hamlet calls it "thinking too precisely on the event." From now on Hamlet to a great extent forgets his uncle and his father's admonition as his meditations cling with tenacious gloom to thoughts of the sinful woman he has found his mother to be.

He kept to his mourning garb largely through loyalty to his father and perhaps partly through a stubborn protest. The mourning raiment meant nothing to him for, as he told his mother, he had a sorrow within which put to shame any outward show of grief, and the black garments were only the frippery and empty display of woe.

However, in spite of his paralysis of will in connection with the "duty" laid upon him by the Ghost, Hamlet is not insensitive to his surroundings. He is alert to much that is going on. He ferrets out the secret of Rosencrantz and Guildenstern. He is quick to catch the contrast between the actor's feigned feelings and his own apathy. He quickly grasps at the plan of using the actors to catch the conscience of the King. But when the actors are gone he says, "Now I am alone." He has come to find a kind of enjoyment in being alone with his own thoughts, and he easily slips back into his melancholy groove of reflection. He berates himself for being a rogue and peasant slave. He muses on the actor's ability to throw himself into his part and weep real tears for Hecuba, who was nothing to him. In this actor's ability to force his feelings into an acting part, he finds something remiss in his own inability to force himself into action instead of unpacking his heart with words when he should have fattened all the vultures in the region with the entrails of the bloody, bawdy, remorseless, treacherous, lecherous, unnatural villain, Claudius.

While Hamlet is planning for the play which is to catch the conscience of the King, we find that, in asking his participation in the experiment, he has given his entire confidence to Horatio and has received in return an earnest response which is an intrinsic part of the constant loyalty of his former school-fellow. This finding of one person whom he can implicitly trust may be said to be a turning point in the play. It is not the climax that is always sought by scholars and usually occurs in the third act. That technical or structural climax in this play comes a little later when Hamlet finds the King praying and slowly draws his sword only to sheathe it a moment later and say, "Up, sword and know a more horrid hent," or when Hamlet deliberately turns from his best opportunity to perform the "task" laid upon him by his father. But the finding of one thoroughly trustworthy friend— one out of the entire population of Denmark—is such a distinct turning point in the mental condition of Hamlet that it might be declared that Horatio saved Hamlet's sanity.

Horatio has not always had full justice at the hands of the critics, but his faithful cooperation with Hamlet in his hour of need is undoubtedly one of the psychological turning points in the play. Another will be found in Hamlet's conversation with his mother in her closet.

In the scene where the players make their appearance, we

find Hamlet in a lighter mood than any which occurs in the play, except, perhaps, the scene with Osric which is somewhat brief. True, as soon as he is alone he begins to reproach himself for his inactivity and expresses admiration for the actor who can so effectively force his feelings, but the soliloquy has not the weariness of life and longing for death that we find elsewhere, even though he does review his situation, reminding himself that he has a dear father murdered and is prompted to revenge by heaven and hell; yet so far he has unpacked his heart only with words. When he hits upon the idea of using the play to trap the King into revealing himself, he is full of eagerness to try his plan; and we can picture him leaving the room with long, quick strides, perhaps snapping his fingers as he says, with enthusiasm, "The play's the thing with which I'll catch the conscience of the King!"

But so deep-seated is his melancholy that in the very next scene, and before the play comes off we find his most despondent soliloquy, the one in which, scholars agree, he most seriously considers the desirability of committing suicide. It is the "To be or not to be" soliloquy. In his first soliloquy when he was wishing his too, too solid flesh would melt, he is still under the shock of his father's death and his mother's marriage. In this later soliloquy he is examining his own mind and the effects of thinking too precisely on the event. He inquires whether it is nobler to suffer the slings and arrows of outrageous Fortune or to take arms against a sea of troubles and by opposing end them. In other words, he is asking whether it is nobler for the mind to wrestle interminably with the unthinkable punishments which outrageous Fortune is hurling upon him or to take the easiest way out by ending his life. Which is the better course, he is asking. He has found something ignoble in letting his mind dwell on the corrupt conditions in the court of Elsinore, of which he is a victim, and is wondering if it would not be more honorable to end it all with a bare bodkin. Then his mind turns to the death that he would bring upon himself. We know not what dreams may come in that sleep of death, he says, and the dread of what may come after death puzzles the will and makes us bear the afflictions we have rather than to fly to other possible evils that we know nothing of. Unfortunately, in this long passage, Shakespeare has attributed to Hamlet a knowledge of some adversities that could not have been a part of his experiences. They were things which Shakespeare himself might have known—the proud man's contumely, the law's delay, etc. Those lines obscure the meaning of the speech and confuse the reader. The average reader may make some such homely substitute as the trials and problems that come to the average individual. To be sure some of Shakespeare's matchless lines will be lost, but they are there to be read though not as a part of Hamlet's experience. Before leaving this soliloquy the thought must be emphasized that "To be or not to be" does not mean, as is commonly thought, "Shall I or shall I not commit suicide?" Hamlet's thought is more elevated than that. He is examining two courses of action to find which is more noble. Which is the nobler course, he is asking, to continue in the mental round, thinking only of the suffering Fortune has brought upon him or to find release by ending his life. The word Fortune is used frequently by Shakespeare as personified Fortune. She is described as fickle, tormenting, smiling, friendly, skittish, blind, malicious. Many other adjectives are used, but it is given to Hamlet to use the strong word "outrageous"—outrageous Fortune.

When the play within the play is over and Hamlet finds the King in an attitude of prayer, or perhaps we might say making an effort at prayer, he recognizes that this is the best opportunity he has had to fulfill his promise to his father. Yet he decides not to take advantage of the situation. Too much has been written about this decision, and arguments have been built up to prove that Hamlet shrinks from performing his duty, or permits his weakened will to sway him. Read with no knowledge of the commentators and their theories, the average student will be of the opinion that Hamlet means what he says. He will not give Claudius the advantage which Claudius denied his brother, and Hamlet's father, the privilege of preparing himself for death. Evidently Hamlet thinks Claudius' prayer is genuine and would prepare Claudius for the hereafter. He will not grant him that benefit, Hamlet says, but will take him at some time when he is as ill-prepared as was his brother, sleeping unsuspectingly in his garden. Many things in Shakespeare must not be measured by the standards of our time. The entire conception of revenge belongs to the thinking of another age, and we must accept these standards or the play falls apart.

When the Prince leaves the kneeling King, he goes immediately to his mother's closet. Hamlet has been reproved for the language he uses to his mother in this scene. It must be kept in mind that the very thought of his mother in the incestuous marriage relation with his uncle has been so abhorrent to him that ugly words have formed themselves in his mind ready to be spewed out at the slightest provocation.

In the scene with his mother we find what some modern scholars consider the psychological climax of the play. After Hamlet's accusations and denunciations the Queen appears to repent of her conduct. Whether we are impressed or not Hamlet genuinely believes that her conscience is moved, and we have evidence later that she turns to Hamlet against the King. But, more important, Hamlet is convinced that she was not implicated in his father's murder. Hamlet's melancholy begins to diminish immediately. This, then, is the psychological turn in Hamlet's mental condition. After this scene he is active and alert, and there is only an occasional trace of melancholy. If his death had not followed so soon after this interview, it seems possible that his normal attitude toward his fellow men would have been restored.

Then Claudius decides to make a second attempt on the life of Hamlet. (The interrupted trip to England has been omitted as having little relevance to Hamlet's mental condition.) Claudius enlists the cooperation of Laertes, and the resulting tragedy is known to any reader. Instead of a defeated, dead Hamlet and a triumphant Claudius securely seated on the throne the room is strewn with corpses as the play closes.

With his last breath Hamlet begs Horatio to tell his story lest a wounded name should live behind him. We may be sure that Horatio would give an accurate, sympathetic account of Hamlet's problem.

But there is a side of Hamlet's story that has not been sufficiently explored and emphasized. As has been pointed out, perhaps too insistently, in this study reams of paper have been consumed in the discussion of Hamlet's delay. Wise and absurd angles of the subject have been explored sometimes tediously and often interestingly. But far, far more important than this century-long controversy about why Hamlet failed to obey the Ghost's instructions (or why he procrastinated, if you insist) is the question; Why did Life strike him down soon after he had crossed the threshold into manhood?

We see him entering the arena of Life, tall, handsome, the observed of all observers, his head high, strong in the belief that man is a wonderful piece of work fresh from the hand of his Creator; He is so noble in reason, even like an angel in his actions; he is the beauty of the world, the paragon of animals. Then in an incredibly short time Life has beaten Hamlet to his knees, and we ask, Why? Why? The answer is to be found in one word, and that word is the name of a woman— Gertrude. Here we come once more to Shakespeare's abiding belief that there are moral laws laid down for us in this life, and that the person who transgresses those laws brings down sorrow not only on his own head but on the heads of others.

Gertrude was too shallow and self-centered to value the devotion of the man who had loved her for many years. Looking into his eyes she could scarcely have failed to see a love that was, as he himself said, "of that dignity that it went hand in hand with the vows [he] made her in marriage." She may have seen only the plentiful sprinkling of silver in her husband's once black hair. Perhaps her vanity led her to believe that she could be attractive to a man younger than herself. Then she looked into the bold, inviting eyes of Claudius —looked and responded, and Claudius had "won to his shameful lust" a "most seeming virtuous queen"—again quoting her husband. She gave little thought to what her flagrantly shameful conduct would do to her husband, and later to her son. She was so lacking in any sense of decency and understanding that she had no conception of the fineness of the son she had borne, even thinking, perhaps, in her vanity that he among all the others would admire her for what she thought was her perpetual youthfulness. She was too unrefined and sensual to realize how revolting her actions would be to her son, once he had grasped the situation between her and his uncle. Yes, Gertrude the weakling who was entirely lacking in moral stamina was as much the cause of the tragedy in *Hamlet* as Iago was the cause of the tragedy in *Othello*.

And what of the character flaw which may have caused Hamlet's downfall for which scholars have searched so long only to have one theory after another discarded and perhaps discredited? As I see it there is no character blemish but rather a rare character perfection. And this character perfection is distinguished by a strong idealism which causes him to view man as a piece of work to be marvelled at because this paragon of animals is so noble in reason. Then he finds his own mother to be guilty of conduct that a beast without the power of reason would have shunned. As a result of this discovery, the earth became to him a foul and pestilent congregation of vapors and the world an unweeded garden where only things rank and vile could grow. Thus we find, at least I find, Hamlet to be a man with ideals so lofty, with heart and mind so tenaciously true to these ideals that he can find no peace and no place in an imperfect world.

MACBETH

MACBETH

M<small>ANY</small> <small>MURDERS</small> are committed in this play, all but the first of them instigated by one man, but it is not, as is too commonly thought, the story of a murderer. If that had been the case, it would not have outlived its author. Shakespeare would not have wasted his time writing a play on such a commonplace and shallow theme as that of a man murdering a king in order to take his throne. That is not the stuff of which great tragedy is made. Briefly stated, and with elaborations to follow, *Macbeth* is the story of a kindly, upright man who was incited and goaded, by the woman he deeply loved, into committing a murder and then, because of his sensitive nature, was unable to bear the heavy burden of guilt that descended upon him as a result of that murder. He became a great sufferer, and because of his mental torment and the fear and suspicion which accompanied it, he went on and on into a life of crime. Muddy thinking, careless reading and reading with preconceived ideas have badly distorted the interpretation of this play. If we could read the play fresh from its first printing, with no advance notices of its contents, very few discerning readers would see it as merely the story of a murderer.

Macbeth's first reaction to the Witches' prophecy is fear. It is Banquo who comments on it. Banquo is a soldier and knows fear when he sees it. This fear is a most important point to be considered in the study of the play. In fact, the entire interpretation of the character of Macbeth hinges on it. Shakespeare has not used the word "fear" carelessly. It should be noted that Macbeth shows no surprise at the Witches' prophecy. The thought is not new to him. It has been broached to him before.

As most readers of the play will recall, Macbeth at some time swore a terrible oath—a vow that he would kill his cousin, King Duncan. It is essential to the understanding of the play to try to determine the time of the swearing of this oath. Some of the older critics placed the time before the opening of the play. If that were the case, if Macbeth had already sworn to kill King Duncan, would his reaction to the Witches' prophecy have been fear? Would it not, rather, have been some form of exultation? May we not reasonably begin to suspect that the suggestion of murder has been made to him, even urged upon him, that he has refused to consider it, and that on hearing the Witches' prophecy he fears for himself, fears that he will break his own resolution, fears that the strong importuning that he has turned aside will eventually win his consent to the direful deed? That he has resisted the temptation up to this time seems clearly revealed in the suddenness with which fear takes possession of him.

Some of the critics have suggested that the oath was sworn after Scene V, Act I, following the home-coming of Macbeth and before the banquet in honor of Duncan. This seems the most logical suggestion and will be discussed later. In the hysterical speech where Lady Macbeth dwells so vehemently on the oath, she makes two other statements that must be considered in all their aspects and in their proper places. One statement is that Macbeth had agreed to do what she was urging but had made the excuse that the time and place were not propitious (did not adhere). This excuse could not have been offered after the return to Inverness because at that time the opportunity for carrying out the plan was virtually in their hands. If they willed it so, the hour of Duncan's death was about to strike. Therefore, it would seem evident that the excuse must have been offered before the play begins.

The third of the three statements is that he broke the enterprise to her. But more of that later.

So, at the opening of the play we have a Macbeth who has sworn no oath but has made the excuse that the time and place for the murder are not favorable. After the Witches' appearance we have a Macbeth deeply perturbed and bewildered by the prophecy. We have a Macbeth who says in soliloquy that the very suggestion of murder is a horrid image that unfixes his hair and makes his securely lodged heart knock at his ribs against the very design of nature. Such thoughts of murder as he has entertained (at his wife's urgency, we learn later) are so unreal and fantastic that they shake his whole state of man with the result that action is choked by imagination. After this review of his feelings we have, at the end of the soliloquy, a Macbeth who stands his ground firmly and says emphatically and fearlessly that if Chance would have him king then Chance may crown him with no effort on his part.

At Forres, Duncan greets Macbeth as his worthiest cousin. The word "cousin" was commonly used in Shakespeare's time to designate any blood relative. In this case, it was used accurately because Duncan and Macbeth were first cousins. Their respective mothers were sisters, daughters of the late King Malcolm. Duncan's mother is mentioned first by Holinshed, and we may conclude that she was the older of the two.

In reading Shakespeare's historical plays, the plays whose stories are founded largely on history or historical legend, care must be taken to guard against confusing the historical character with the character as Shakespeare presents it. History deals with facts and factual events. Shakespeare goes beyond events and delves into the motives of the people participating in them. His characters often differ markedly from the personages of history. However, as a little side remark, one may credibly contend that the student is sometimes warranted in recalling that the more intelligent of Shakespeare's audience knew his source material (the histories and stories from which he took his plots), and that Shakespeare seems at times to have taken for granted the audience's familiarity with the story.

In the case of Duncan, we find Holinshed telling us plainly that he had "small skill in warlike affairs," and that the rebellion of Macdonwald and the invasion of Sweno had "chanced through the feeble and slothful administration of Duncan." Shakespeare omits to mention the weaknesses of Duncan but stresses his gentleness and apparent kindliness. As a result, the critics have represented the murder of Duncan as being particularly shocking because of these amiable qualities. Not enough stress has been laid upon Duncan's unaccountably sudden and arbitrary appointment of Malcolm to the royal succession in the very hour of Macbeth's triumph, the hour when he came to report to his King that he had successfully defended the throne from a Scottish rebel and from a foreign invader. Duncan owed the security of his throne to Macbeth and to Macbeth alone. Whether we see the action of Duncan as the overbearing attitude of an autocrat or the unthinking deed of a weakling, it would be difficult to avoid the conclusion that the appointment is made at this time in order to diminish the stature of Macbeth and to minimize the importance of his great victories. The affront to Macbeth, or the insult to Macbeth (as it may appear to different minds), cannot be overemphasized. Also, note must be made of the fact that Duncan was taking the law into his own hands in making this appointment because, according to Holinshed, "the ordinance was that if he that should succeed were not of able age to take the charge upon himself, he that was next of blood should be admitted." Perhaps Shakespeare was taking for granted that his audience knew that the historian had said, "Duncan did what in him lay to defraud him [Macbeth] of all manner of titles and claims, which might in time to come pretend to the crown." Malcolm was under age, and this fact made Macbeth first heir to the throne.

In the play Duncan's reception of Macbeth seems to be unnecessarily formal. It seems to be lacking in any genuine or enthusiastic appreciation of what Macbeth has done. It appears to have no note of cordiality. The contention may be made that the language of the court was necessarily formal, but William Shakespeare knew how to put warmth even into a formal speech. Duncan really promises Macbeth nothing. Macbeth's replies are stiff and formal, showing an outer conformity to the demands of the occasion, but they are stilted and unenthusiastic. Just what Macbeth expected of Duncan, if anything, in the way of reward for his services is impossible to say, but we may be sure he expected an honest praise for his victories. These things he does not receive. Duncan's mild, patronizing manner must have been gall and wormwood to a man who had seen what Macbeth had seen that day.

In the aside which Macbeth speaks after the appointment of Malcolm, Macbeth seems to show himself as a man of sudden and violent temper. Duncan's complete lack of appreciation of what he has done and the degradation which this weak cousin has heaped upon him aroused in Macbeth a raging fury. In his soliloquy, all the dangerous thoughts which he has repressed and kept under command of his will break forth in a torrent of awesome, horrifying words that make one's blood run cold as they depict the horrible deed he is vowing to commit. In this fiery speech he is letting his imagination play with the thought of committing the deed, but there seems to be no fixed determination to do it.

Scholars have sometimes speculated as to whether Shakespeare did not occasionally pen a speech for the sake of giving the actor who was to deliver it a good bit of acting. Richard Burbage would have "brought down the house" with this speech. From this time on his lines in the play will be tinged with sadness. This was the last chance for such a rousing speech and so perhaps Shakespeare—but who knows? And he did the same thing for John Lowin, the young man who played the part of Iago. In the midst of his most despicable scene, he is given that gem of philosophical wisdom, beginning "Who steals my purse steals trash."

And the man who speaks this terrifying speech is the same man who, a few hours ago in quiet contemplation said, "If Chance would have me king, why, Chance may crown me without my stir."

Perhaps this is as good a place as any to say frankly that the death of Duncan was not the unprovoked murder of a saintly man, as it is too often represented. Duncan himself was, to some extent at least, responsible for his untimely taking off, because of his calculatingly unfair treatment of a kindly disposed cousin and an intensely loyal subject. This conclusion is based on the facts as represented in Shakespeare's play and not to any appreciable extent on material culled from the pages of Holinshed.

Macbeth's resentment of the injustice of this appointment of Malcolm and the deep, deadly hurt it brought, remain with him to the end of the play. In his latest defiance, he says, "I will not yield, to kiss the ground before young Malcolm's feet." He preferred death to that, and the poignancy of his final reference (after all that had gone between) to the unwarranted wrong the King had done him is one of the most pathetic things in all Shakespeare.

Macbeth's impassioned aside which follows Duncan's announcement of the appointment of Malcolm requires more careful consideration in connection with the theory here advanced. On the surface, it seems to be a sudden outburst of thoughts he has been harboring for a period of time. But certain angles of the situation must be examined. Macbeth would have been less than human if he had not, perhaps frequently, given thought to the favorable side of his wife's urgent arguments. It was true, he would admit, that Duncan was an inept king, that he, Macbeth could fill the office with more ability and greater forcefulness. It was true that Macbeth's claim to the throne was all but equal to that of Duncan, and that Lady Macbeth was of the royal blood of Scotland. It was true that Duncan was getting old, almost in his dotage, while Macbeth was in the prime of life. All these things he was compelled to admit, and these admissions may have been flavored with a temptation to yield to his wife's persuasions. Also, the thought of being king had its attractive side, but it could scarcely have been pronounced enough to constitute a strong temptation. Even though there may have been a mild temptation on the part of Macbeth, it was put aside so decisively and peremptorily as to be of little consequence in evaluating his character. The thought of murdering his own cousin was abhorrent to him from the beginning—the thought of murdering anyone, in fact. So a little earlier, as has been said, when the Witches made their startling promise, he was shaken by the fear that he might yet yield to his wife's incessant appeals.

Now for a few moments following the announcement by Duncan, his better judgment is unseated, and his imagination takes over with a fantastic picture of himself committing the horrible deed that he has pushed aside with such level judgment.

The action of Duncan in appointing Malcolm has received too little careful scrutiny. The character of Duncan has had only superficial consideration. On the surface Duncan is mild and gentle, but mild, gentle people can be envious and malicious. Duncan appears to be both. The thought of his young cousin so outstripping him in valor and becoming the savior of Scotland was more than his weak kingly equanimity could bear. The acclaim of the people expressed in those messages that came "thick as hail" brought a strong impulse of vengeance to his mind, and the result was the appointment of Malcolm to the successor's position in the presence of the group of nobles. One must get the picture clear. Macbeth had not only saved the throne for Duncan. He had dispersed an invading army that would have been the forerunner of an invading people who would have wiped out the lives of many of the Scottish people and changed the lot of the remainder. So what the traditionally mild and kindly Duncan did to Macbeth was almost as cruel as knifing a man in his bed. As has been noted, the hurt of this appointment remains with Macbeth to the end of the play.

The distance from Forres to Inverness is a good forty miles, as the crow flies. As Macbeth mounted his horse with the grace and agility of an expert rider, we may readily believe he was congratulating himself on the fact that he had been able to conceal his inmost thoughts and to say aloud the felicitous things the occasion required. As his horse got under way, his mind must have turned back to his brief interview with the King. What was it that Duncan had been saying about planting someone and watching him grow? Why, it was himself, Macbeth, whom this inconsequential King was promising to plant—Macbeth who had outgrown his elder cousin in every respect, particularly that of soldiering, a long time ago and, he would continue his thinking, Duncan's patronizing generalizations about his intentions were difficult enough to accept—and then that stunning, unbelievable announcement! He had made no inquiries about the battles for the simple reason that he knew too little about military matters to ask intelligent questions. His part in any military engagement was to accept the services of faithful, trained soldiers and appropriate the honors to himself. He had accepted them with his usual urbanity—and then came forth with that incomprehensible pronouncement! Yes, and there were promises to all the thanes, glittering generalities about signs of nobleness that would shine like stars upon all who would deserve them. And these resplendent honors would be bestowed by none other than the great King Duncan himself. Surely a soldier's services were worth more than this flimsy, dubious, unsubstantial, patronizing recognition.

Macbeth's mind would be turned back to the events of the day. Duncan had never set foot on such a battlefield as Macbeth had just seen—was still seeing in his mind in spite of all the things that had come between. There was hand-to-hand fighting with men falling on all sides. The ground soon became soaked with blood, and as the battle went on the blood mixed with the earth became slippery so that a man must watch his footing. Many of the men had come into the fight naked with only their shields before them, and when they were down their stark, sprawling limbs made a grotesque, ugly sight. He shuddered as he recalled how those naked bodies, rigid and distorted in death had a fantastic uncouthness that could not soon be forgotten. As Macbeth ranged the field in search of Macdonwald, he saw men with their brains running out, men with weird grins on their gaunt, dead faces. In some parts of the field there were horses with their great bellies upturned to the skies. Some of them had deep gashes in their sides through which their huge entrails spilled out over an unbelievably large space of ground. The stench became sickening, almost unbearable. The battle was at a stage where it might go to either contestant. And then Macdonwald stood before him. This Macdonwald was aiming to usurp the throne of Scotland, the throne of his grandfather, the great King Malcolm. There was no one else equal to dealing with this ferocious rebel. Banquo was a brave soldier, but he was now past his prime. Macdonwald was a man of mighty strength. Macbeth was in great physical danger. It was now Macbeth or Macdonwald. So Macbeth took his great sword and ripped Macdonwald from the navel to the chin, making sure he missed no vital organ. It was a hideous, gruesome thing to do to any human being, but it was a choice between one individual and his native land. It was all for Scotland and his people.

Altogether it was a foul day except that it ended in a fair victory. He had been saying something of the kind to Banquo as they walked through the woods, for the stench of the battlefield was still in his nostrils, but Banquo was so dog-tired that he could think only of the distance they had yet to go before reaching Forres. Then they had met the Witches. As they continued their journey with Ross and Angus, they must have stopped occasionally to rest. It must have been during one of these rest periods that he wrote the letter to his wife, telling her about the Witches. He had put the letter in his pouch and on reaching Forres had given it to the first messenger he could find. Now, since their stay in Forres had been so short, he might even overtake the messenger. His mind ran back to the reports of Ross and Angus. They had told how messages had come to Duncan by post after post, thick as hail, they had said, and these messages pouring in in such great numbers carried praise of Macbeth and his great defense of the kingdom. Could it be, Macbeth asked himself, that Duncan could not tolerate this voluminous praise of his younger cousin? Macbeth must have knit his brows and wondered.

He wondered, too, if the other thanes had caught the patronizing tone of the King's indefinite, noncommittal promises. And now Duncan was coming to Inverness. He would have some insignificant trinket to present to his hostess, in the condescending way that he had. It would be a precious jewel, to be sure, but it would be a mere bauble compared with the crown jewels she had every right to wear. Yes, the crown jewels belonged to them by right of his victories. In earlier days, kings had won their crowns on the battlefield, in just such battles as he had won this very day. By every law the kingdom had known, he, Macbeth, was king of Scotland!

It should be noted that he makes no plan for getting rid of

Duncan. If he had had any serious intention of murdering Duncan, he would have been full of plans by the time he reached Inverness. At no time does he make one plan or add a single suggestion to the program his wife has laid out.

The cooling breezes from off Moray Firth ruffled his thick, auburn hair and cooled his flushed face. By the time he reached Inverness Castle, he was able to say with every appearance of calmness, "My dearest love, Duncan comes here tonight," and then after her enthusiastic outbreak a still more quiet, "We will speak further."

Obviously the letter which Lady Macbeth reads was written before the meeting with Duncan. There is no evidence of the mental turmoil occasioned by that interview. After his description of the encounter with the Witches, which Lady Macbeth seemingly has read before she enters the room, the writer goes on to say that he has learned from indisputable authority that the Witches have more than mortal knowledge. How and where he has made this discovery is not told. Perhaps he exaggerated a little in order to impress her more deeply and more certainly with the news. Macbeth explains that he has thought it a good thing to send his missive as soon as possible, in order that she may not be deprived of the right of rejoicing by remaining in ignorance of the great news that is in store for her.

This is the first communication of Macbeth with his wife that we have in the play. In this letter we find a great eagerness to share good news with her and a profound assurance that she will not only understand and welcome it but will rejoice with him. Here is a suggestion of a devoted companionship, a wish on his part to merit her approval and a desire on his part to make an apparently improbable thing seem credible or, to phrase it differently, an attempt on his part to avoid the suspicion of using his imagination too freely. Already we see him living up to the standards of his more practical wife. It should be remembered that at the time of the letter writing the impediment of Malcolm's appointment had not yet crossed his path. There is no evidence in the letter that he sees Duncan's murder as the only way to the throne. That purpose only begins to take form in the perturbation with which he speaks his aside before leaving the presence of Duncan. This is not the case with Lady Macbeth as evidenced in her determined, passionate response to the letter. Another conclusion that may be drawn from the letter is that any ambition either of them had is for both. Their marriage had been one of perfect teamwork up to the time of her "breaking the enterprise" to him.

Leaving the continuity of the story as must occasionally be done in such a sketch as this, one is reminded that Dr. Marc Parrott says that there is not a shred of evidence that Lady Macbeth is ambitious for herself. One wonders if the good doctor has overlooked the lines:

> . . . you shall put
> This night's great business into my dispatch
> Which shall to all our nights and days to come
> Give solely sovereign sway and masterdom.

Do not these lines include more than a shred of ambition for herself? No, this calculating, vociferous lady was not naive enough to overlook the fact that once Macbeth became king she automatically became queen.

It must have been a small secluded room free from interruptions and intrusions where they met to "speak further." There he would tell her of the battles and of the meeting with Duncan. He would speak vehemently of the King's shallow, indefinite promises, and he would tell her of the appointment of Malcolm. All the rage that had been welling up in him would come to the surface as he told that story under her compelling urgency. This was her opportunity to do as she had promised herself she would do after she had read the letter—to pour her spirits in his ear, to chasten with the valor of her tongue all that might impede him from the golden crown. We may be sure she took this opportunity to use all her monstrous powers of persuasion. Thus he goaded himself, or was goaded by his wife, into swearing the terrible oath, whether he had any clear purpose of keeping it or not.

Many scholars have suggested that Macbeth watched the arrival of Duncan from an upper window because he did not feel equal to playing the part of the cordial host. I can picture him standing at that window overlooking the entrance with a scowl on his face. As Duncan, Banquo, Macduff and others come up the path after leaving their horses to the grooms, I can hear him saying, "Yes, he is making some insipid remark about those birds winging their way home to their nests. He has no conception of what some of us have experienced this day."

The atmosphere of the banquet where they met in honor of Duncan must have been a normal, happy one. As Macbeth looks about the table the gracious Duncan, and Duncan could be gracious, is basking in the hospitality of his hostess. Keyed up as she is, Lady Macbeth is exceptionally cordial to all her guests. His partner, Banquo, is in good spirits enjoying the pleasures of the festive board after a fatiguing day, and his good friend Macduff is saying that, now that the wars are over, he must be getting back home to Fife, to his wife and children, whom he has the habit of calling affectionately his little chicks. The environment is not one to lend itself to thoughts of murder. Macbeth becomes uncontrollably nervous and leaves the room. In the bustle outside the banquet room where divers servants pass over the stage with dishes and services, we are vouchsafed the privilege of visualizing Macbeth for one brief moment with troops of friends who have always been a delight to him and who have formed a large part of his dreams of the future. It is only for a brief moment that we are permitted to indulge in that mental picture.

Outside the banquet room where the atmosphere of friendship has cleared his mind of its horrible imaginings, he is trying desperately to see the situation from a practical viewpoint. In his soliloquy, we find him saying first that if the deed were effectively accomplished then it were best it should be done quickly. He muses for a moment on the consequences and then gives five reasons for not committing the murder. First, he says that if we view the situation from the limitations of this life, we are taking no heed of the life to come. Second, in addition to this we shall have judgment here. Third, Duncan is here in his own castle in double trust; Macbeth is his kinsman and, also, his subject. Both of these trusts are strong reasons against the performance of the deed. As Duncan's host he should shut the door against the murderer, not bear the sword himself. Fourth, Duncan has borne himself so well and has been so blameless in the performance of his great office that his virtues will plead to the people like the tongues of angels against the deep damnation of his murder. Fifth, he, Macbeth, has no spur to prick the sides of his intent except his own vaulting ambition which is in danger of overleaping itself like a rider vaulting too far over his horse and falling on the other side.

It should be noted that in this soliloquy, there is not a word about the appointment of Malcolm and no mention of any oath he has made. All the rancor has disappeared, and the oath he has sworn in the presence of his wife has become incongruous in the radiant warmth of friendship.

He has admitted to a vaulting ambition. We have no other evidence of personal ambition except, possibly, his own word in this speech. Onrushing events crowd the thought out of his mind and out of our view. We do have ample evidence of his ambition for his family, ambition for a son who might succeed him. The matter of Macbeth's thinking in terms of dynasty does not occur readily to the student of today, because of our removal from the times when building a dynasty

was all important to a noble house. These things were familiar to all the people of Shakespeare's time. We think normally
of ambition as a personal thing, but it is not always so. Macbeth's stupendous imagination, as revealed later in the play,
gives him a breadth of vision altogether out of keeping with
a narrow, personal ambition.

When Lady Macbeth appears from the banquet room, we
learn that he has again decided to proceed no further with
the business. He tells her so definitely. He wishes to bask in
the honors he has received from the King and in the golden
opinions of the people which he has won in battle. He does
not wish to put these honors aside too soon. The first part of
his excuse is flimsy and weak because the King has not covered him with honors except one inherited advancement and
one not very important promotion. Note should be taken of
the fact that these excuses offered to his wife do not resemble in any degree the thoughts he expressed in his own
meditative soliloquy. One might reasonably ask if he thought
she would understand only practical reasons, that his real reasons were beyond her comprehension.

In her hysterical answer to his decision, Lady Macbeth
makes one of her three statements already mentioned where
she asks what beast it was that made him break the enterprise to her. She herself said, in substance, that they had
talked the matter over, but he was too full of the milk of
human kindness to catch the nearest way to the throne, by
the murder of Duncan. He was not without ambition, she
had said, but lacked the wickedness ("illness")[1] that should
accompany this ambition and make it possible for him to
commit the murder. And he had argued that the time was not
propitious. Later, in the presence of his great anger, in that
small room, she could easily have convinced herself that he
had broken the enterprise to her. Also, there was the letter
telling of the Witches which she might, with no foundation

[1] G. B. Harrison notes.

whatsoever, have interpreted into breaking the enterprise to her. A careful reading of that letter finds no suggestion that the throne is to be reached by foul means. But the letter suggests the use of foul means to the reader, Lady Macbeth, to the extent that she pictures herself doing the deed with a keen knife while she implores the heavens not to peep through the blanket of the dark to cry, "Hold, hold."

A woman who could speak as Lady Macbeth does, who could call upon the spirits that tend on mortal thoughts to unsex her and fill her from head to foot full of direct cruelty, who could entreat these same spirits to stop all avenues of remorse so that no compunctions of conscience will interfere with the carrying out of her purpose, who could call upon the night to wrap itself in the murkiest, gloomiest smoke of hell in order to hide, even from the keen knife she would use, the wound she would make when she herself stabs the sleeping King, such a terrible, frightful woman would not scruple at telling a little wife-to-husband lie to accomplish her purpose. Besides, from time immemorial women have used the trick of making a man think that the thing she wants was his plan in the first place.[1]

Surely it is not too fanciful or sentimental to suggest that she touched his Achilles heel when she reflected on his courage—courage of a dauntless soldier who had accomplished almost miraculous feats of bravery that very day. She had courage but of a different kind—courage to take events into her own hands, courage to interfere with the workings of Providence itself in order to gain the thing she was so violently bent on attaining. He did not have that kind of courage. His courage was that of physical prowess, the determined will to risk his life to right a wrong. When she so convincingly outlined the practical details of her plan, he

[1] I was pleased to hear Bishop Sheen say that he could not find himself committing the speeches of Lady Macbeth to memory—as if they would defile his mind. I have forgotten how he expressed the thought. He knew most of Macbeth's lines.

stood in amazed admiration of her daring fortitude. He was so deeply stirred by her dauntless spirit that he cried in bewildered amazement, "Bring forth men children only." Thus he had succumbed at last to her persuasion.

And now William Shakespeare is about to show us once more the results that inevitably follow when little man steps into the role of Providence and takes upon himself the divine prerogatives and the responsibility of guiding the destinies of his fellow men.

But the struggle and the suffering of Macbeth has never been sufficiently emphasized by commentators. The terrifying experience with the dagger is not merely an effective piece of play acting. It is an agonizing experience to him while it lasts, but after that terrifying, intolerable moment, he is able to curb his wild imagination and recognize that there is no such thing as the bloody dagger marshalling him the way he was to go. It is the bloody business they have talked about that has given form to the dagger.

On his way to the chamber of the sleeping King, Macbeth's thought is only for the man whose soul he is about to send to heaven or to hell.

And now the deed is done. By the eerie light of a flickering night-candle Macbeth stands in paralyzed horror as the blood spurts, then flows thin trickles from the side of the stricken King. Strange, he must have been thinking, how the body takes on its inanimate, clod-like appearance immediately the spark of life has departed. And this inert, board-like thing was, until a few moments ago, his cousin Duncan, his big cousin whom he had admired and idealized as a boy. Duncan had become a king, a kindly king, but now——

From a room close by comes the sound of sleepy laughter, and he thinks he hears someone say "Murder." The sleepers mutter their prayers. One says, "God bless us" and the other says, "Amen." Macbeth attempts to repeat the "Amen," for he suddenly realizes his great need for blessing, but the word

"Amen" sticks in his throat. Then he thinks he hears a voice say, "Sleep no more, Macbeth does murder sleep." The voice grows louder and louder and cries to all the house, "Sleep no more, Glamis has murdered sleep and therefore Cawdor shall sleep no more. Macbeth shall sleep no more." With this voice of doom ringing in his ears, he manages to stumble down the stairs into the presence of his wife.

It must be remembered, repeated and never forgotten so long as the story is under consideration that the man who descends that stairway has lost, or thinks he has lost, his immortal soul. This terrifying, haunting thought will never leave him. It will be present in varying degrees throughout his lifetime, or throughout the play. It will fill his mind with scorpions. It will drive him to remove one and then another from his path, not in order that he may continue occupying the throne but that he may once again know safety and peace. This obsessing thought will be beside his bed at night telling him he shall never know again the healing balm of sleep, kind nature's sweet restorer, all because he has lost contact with his Maker. Macbeth speaks openly of this only once after that dreadful night when he says (in Act III, Scene I) that he has given his "eternal jewel" to Satan in order to make the seeds of Banquo kings. Commentators have universally agreed that "eternal jewel" means immortal soul. In these days of careless or indifferent thinking about religion, it is difficult to conceive what it meant in the early days of Christianity for a man to think he had lost his immortal soul.

Lady Macbeth has expected to see him descend the stairs quickly and cautiously, showing a little nervousness, to be sure, but infinitely relieved that the deed has been done. Instead, she is dumfounded by his changed appearance. She scarcely recognizes him and can only exclaim, "My husband!" He tries to tell her how he has cut himself off from all Christian mankind so that when other men pray he cannot respond with the customary "Amen." (The critics who have insisted that he had a fear-ridden conscience have taken too little note of this sensitive Christian conscience.) Already his imagination is prodding him with thoughts that are unbearable. Thus before he descended the stairs his great suffering had begun. As the scene closes a deep abyss of regret and remorse has opened before him sweeping him into its unfathomable depths as he utters that hauntingly touching line, "Wake Duncan with thy knocking. I would thou couldst." The murder of Duncan has been to him a soul-shaking thing. It would not have been so if he had been the instigator of the crime.

The hushed awesomeness of the second scene of Act II can be found only in the lines Shakespeare has written, but the picture it carries of Macbeth's completely undone condition lingers with the reader long after the actual words have slipped from memory. Its heartbreak is renewed with each successive reading.

The murder of the grooms is of more importance than may appear on the surface. With the killing of the grooms Macbeth begins to lie and dissemble. The man who only a few hours ago was most sincere and truthful has now plunged into the depths of duplicity. He is caught in that deadly maelstrom which William Butler Yates called "the whirlpool of insincerity from which no man returns." Consciously or unconsciously he becomes cunning and calculating, counting on the killing of the supposed murderers to impress upon his hearers the great depth of his love for Duncan. He overacts the part, and his speech about his "violent love" for Duncan seems full of bombast. Lady Macbeth detects the bombast and the deceit. Or, there is a possibility that the turmoil of his overwrought mind and his always overactive imagination might momentarily have pictured the grooms as the actual killers. (Lady Macbeth had smeared them with blood and had defied anyone to believe otherwise than that they were the murderers.) Macbeth had no genuine fear of the grooms. At the time of the murder they were in a death-like sleep, and in a normal mental condition he would have been well aware of this fact. Any fear he may have entertained came from his wild uncontrollable imagination.

Lady Macbeth is basically a sincere person. In her lonely hours at Inverness Castle, she has permitted her thinking to run to dreams of royalty until she is willing to "catch the nearest way," but she respects and delights in the honor of her lord. The killing of the grooms and the brazen excuses he offers are so foreign to his better nature that she quails at the sight of what she has done to him just as he has quailed before the deed he has done. She knows now that he will never be able to carry through their plan and assume the role of king as she undoubtedly could have assumed that of queen. At this juncture Lady Macbeth faints, and the fainting is genuine. It comes from her sudden realization of the terrible thing she has done to the man she genuinely loves. Her mistake was in not recognizing the extreme sensitiveness of this strong man. If Macbeth had been less sensitive, if he had not possessed that far-reaching imagination that had so fatally told him that he has isolated himself from all Christian mankind (a pariah in fact) he might have stopped with the murder of Duncan, justifying the act, if necessary, on the ground that he could fill the office with greater efficiency and usefulness to the country. Lady Macbeth's fainting is the beginning of her nervous breakdown. And Macbeth has begun to play a part, a part he will carry with varying degrees of success to the end except when his nervous system rebels, as it does in the banquet scene that was supposed to honor Banquo.

Besides Lady Macbeth, the one who knows how much Macbeth is acting is Banquo. In the scene where Banquo is starting for his afternoon ride, the conversation between the new King and his "chief guest" is artificial on both sides. In pretending that he is about to seek advice from Banquo, Macbeth has sunk a little lower in the art of brazen deception, and when he tells of the young princes' sojourn in England and Ireland, where they are filling their hearers with "strange inventions," he is relying on the security of his office to prevent a contradiction from Banquo. A few lines farther on he says that his fears in Banquo sink deep.

In the long soliloquy, beginning "To be thus is nothing," he reflects that Banquo would dare a great deal, and yet his daring is accompanied by a certain wisdom that would guide him to act safely. So he is a man to be feared. Macbeth has come to believe that his own genius is rebuked by Banquo, as it is said Mark Antony's was by Augustus Caesar.[1] Then, like a cog slipping naturally into its own notch, his thoughts turn to the Witches and their prophecy, and he concludes that he has defiled his mind for the descendants of Banquo; he has murdered the gracious Duncan for them; he has poisoned his own peace of mind and given his immortal soul (eternal jewel) to the devil, the common enemy of man— all this to make the descendants of Banquo kings! Rather than face such an outcome, he challenges Fate to enter the lists with him against Banquo and champion him to the last extremity, even though that extremity be death itself. This deep regret about poisoning his peace of mind and losing his immortal soul has become his crying lament.

It is important to note how often he speaks of what is happening to his mind. His mind slipped from its moorings on the night of Duncan's murder, and he became bewildered because he could not say "Amen." Now he sees his mind defiled and irretrievably sullied, all to no avail. Before long we shall find another striking statement about what is happening to his mind.

The conversation with the two murderers (of Banquo)

[1] Some years ago, I read in a newspaper that a museum (in Chicago, as I recall) had received, from Egypt, a set of loaded dice which were thought to have belonged to Julius Caesar, and I found myself wondering if Julius had passed them along to Augustus.

should be compared with the soliloquy Macbeth speaks before the murder of Duncan. In that earlier speech, he names five reasons why the murder should not be committed. He emphasizes the virtues of the meek and gentle Duncan, weighs his own responsibilities as kinsman and host, and speaks disparagingly of his own eager ambitions. He even omits to mention (having forgotten it for the moment) the appointment of Malcolm as Prince of Cumberland. Now, before the murder of Banquo, he lies to the two underworld characters, telling them that Banquo is their enemy, defaming his character and giving lame excuses for not performing the deed himself. The man, who a short time ago was full of human kindness, has become cruel, cowardly, and unscrupulous. So far has his character disintegrated.

In the conversation with his wife immediately following the interview with the murderers, he speaks in terrifying words of the danger they are in because the snake they have intended to kill is only scotched and will recover to become a menace to them. He turns defiant and dares both heaven and earth. He flouts the universe itself, saying it may become disjointed before they will eat their meals in fear and sleep under the scourge of the terrible dreams that shake them night after night. Sadly he reflects that it would be better to be with the dead (Duncan) whom they have sent to eternal peace, with the thought of gaining earthly satisfaction for themselves, than to lie in frenzied restlessness as if they were on a rack. Duncan is in his grave, he says mournfully. After life's fitful fever he sleeps well. The treason of his own (Macbeth's) act has done its worst on Duncan, and now neither the steel sword that was used nor the poison that was contemplated can touch him further. Also, the dead man is forever removed from the disquieting anxieties of civil and foreign wars. Gradually he is sinking into a melancholy mood which is descending upon him like a thick, enveloping fog.

At his wife's admonition, he tries to show an interest in the forthcoming banquet, but in urging her to make Banquo pre-eminent in her attention he is speaking a lie, because he knows that Banquo will not be present. Then, recoiling from the deception that must be practiced and the horrible deed he is contemplating, he breaks forth in startling suddenness with the anguished cry, "O, full of scorpions is my mind, dear wife!" The intense pain caused by the sting of the scorpion is proverbial, and Macbeth is saying that his terrifying thoughts are like a swarm of scorpions with innumerable sharp points that stab ruthlessly, relentlessly, and unceasingly at his mental peace. This line is unquestionably the most pathetic and moving one in the play.

As they talk about Banquo and Fleance, he tells her with dreamy gloom that before the daytime creatures have found their resting-places there will be done a deed of dreadful significance. He goes to the window, and, as he watches the shadows gather, he again loses himself in his own thoughts. He speaks to the night, bidding it come down and blind the tender eyes of pitying day and, with its bloody and invisible hand, cancel and tear to pieces the bond between destiny and the house of Banquo, as revealed by the Witches. (Again that note of fear of Banquo's progeny!) It is that great bond that keeps him pale, he declares. He notices the crow winging its way to the rooky wood. His fancy sees the good things of daytime sinking to sleep, and he remarks that the black operators of night now arouse themselves to pursue their prey. He has completely shut his wife out of his confidence and has identified himself with the night's black agents.

His anxiety to be rid of Fleance still further emphasizes the theory that Macbeth was ambitious only to found a dynasty. There is no reason to suppose that he has any fear of Fleance as he has of Banquo. Fleance is a mere boy, and Banquo would be less likely to confide in him any suspicion he may have had than to confide in other men of the Court. It is, then, the fear of Fleance as the father of a line of kings that prompts the attempt to get rid of him. His desire to be rid of Fleance has nothing to do with the fears that "stick deep" in Banquo. It has to do with his dreams of the "imperial theme" while his fears of Banquo center around Banquo's suspicions about the murder of Duncan. Also, Macbeth's ambition to found a dynasty is in keeping with his great breadth of vision. He is not a man of narrow personal ambition.

Up to Act III, Scene IV, Macbeth has thought that the removal of one more person would destroy his fears and rid him of his "horrible imaginings." But in this banquet scene, where the ghost of Banquo appears, those "horrible imaginings" reach their climax. It is a stirring, hair-raising scene with haunting lines. The extent to which his tortured mind has affected his nervous system is vividly shown here. The long, sleepless nights have taken their toll of his strength, and he is physically and mentally unfit to meet the situation.

He has depended on avoiding the actual bloodiness of the murder of Banquo by having the deed executed by others. At the sight of blood on the murderer's face he is completely undone. The "horrible shadow" that rises to mock him is another example of the way his mind can make a realistic picture from a thing that affects him deeply, as in the case of the bloody dagger. His conscience, too, is more active here. He speaks of the time before man-made statutes had outlawed murder, the time when if a man's brains were out they were out and that was the end. This has been interpreted to mean that before the Christian Era murder was not frowned upon, but since the advent of Christianity murder has become a sin. If this is the correct interpretation of the passage, then we must again accord Macbeth a sensitive Christian conscience. This would weigh definitely against the theory advanced by H. B. Charlton that Macbeth's was merely a fear-ridden conscience. Another statement by this eminent scholar is that "Macbeth has sin in his soul; his own evil brings about his doom." [1] Charlton announces himself as a "devout Bradleyite," but contrast this statement with Bradley's paragraph following his quotation of the tomorrow and tomorrow speech: "In the very depths a gleam of his native love of goodness, and with it a touch of tragic grandeur rests upon him. The evil he has desperately embraced continues to madden or to wither his inmost heart. No experience in the world could bring him to glory in it, or to forget what he once was and Iago and Goneril never were." [2]

And Peter Alexander asks this question: "How could a fighter of Macbeth's power, one so eminently suited for rule and homage, be so troubled by Duncan's taking off as never again to be the man he was, but for some profound rightness in his soul, an inexorable goodness that will assert itself the more, the more it is denied?" [3]

Marc Parrott cautions us that "A few words are necessary to clear the character of the hero from current misconceptions. Macbeth is by no means a representative of the old barbaric Highland chieftains, no rough soldier or mere man of action. On the contrary, he is a noble and courteous gentleman, . . . and his hesitation before and his suffering after the murder of Duncan shows how abhorrent such a deed of blood was to his original disposition. His relation to his wife in the first part of the play and his bitter sense of loneliness at the close show him to be a man of warm human affections." [4]

We must never think of Macbeth as a criminal type. If he had been, there would have been no tragedy. If he had been the instigator of the first murder, there would have been no tragedy. The play would have been only the story of the fulfillment of the promise of an evil nature. The tragedy lies

---

[1] H. B. Charlton. *Shakespearean Tragedy*, page 141.
[2] Bradley. *Shakespearean Tragedy*, page 365.
[3] Peter Alexander. *Shakespeare's Life and Art*, page 173.
[4] *Introduction* to Parrott's Edition to the play, page 45.

in the fact that he had no evil tendencies but was trapped into the commission of a revolting crime against his will.

But G. B. Harrison finds Macbeth's character a mixture of good and evil qualities: "He has bravery and nobility counterbalanced by ambition. Above all he has an overpowering imagination which makes him see not only what the results of an action will be, but also its essential meaning. His loyalty and ambition are equally balanced until he comes into the presence of his wife. Lady Macbeth is at the same time greater and lesser than her husband. She has a hardness which he lacks, but she has none of his subtlety and perception. She knows her husband well and despises him a little, but to satisfy her ambition, which is a crude desire to see her man King, she will devote herself soul and body to evil. When Duncan is dead, the contrast between man and wife becomes more vivid. Macbeth is overwhelmed with the significance of his filthy deed. His wife is concerned only with the details of what must be done next—with facts. She has no imagination. The passage between Macbeth and Lady Macbeth after the murder is one of the finest examples of atmosphere ever created in drama." [1] Later, speaking of the sleepwalking scene this understanding scholar says, "The resistance of this hard, practical woman has broken down. *She was the real cause and agent of the tragedy.* [Italics mine.] In the words which she utters in her sleep, she gives her own answer to the casual remark that 'a little water cleanses us of this deed.' This is the true dramatic irony, tragic and terrible, where the easiest remarks have the most ghastly significance and are echoed by a kind of devilish chuckle."

In the last speech in this scene (Act III, Scene IV) Macbeth reveals the fact that his morbidly sensitive mind has added suspicion to fear as he tells of keeping a watch in every house. This seems strange, in view of the fact that only that

[1] G. B. Harrison. *Shakespeare, the Complete Works*, pages 1187-8.

afternoon he had said he feared only Banquo. Was he lying to himself then, or is he now merely saying that it is his intention to place a fee'd servant in every house? And now that suspicion has taken hold of him he recognizes that there is no going back. He pictures himself as being midstream in a river of blood. What a horrible experience was his at that moment!

He has thought that the murder of Banquo would put an end to his fears and, in a sense, that became true, because with the murder of Banquo his fear turned to panic. All the later crimes are committed in a state of panic—panic which later becomes frenzy. The word "panic" is used here with the meaning given by Webster which is as follows: panic— "terror inspired by misapprehension of danger, especially when accompanied by unreasoning and frantic efforts to secure safety."

In this last speech, too, he anticipates the murder of the Macduff family, and the subsequent crimes that are described by Ross in the scene where he joins in the meeting between Macduff and Malcolm. One may ask, without being sentimental, why Shakespeare draws a curtain over these later crimes, presenting them only in dramatic perspective, or in the form of narration. In all the plays, there is nothing like the drawing of this curtain. It is as if Shakespeare were saying, I have shown you enough of the crimes of this misguided, tortured man. He will go on and on to unspeakable crimes, but I shall reveal them to you only by hearsay, and that at a great distance from their perpetration, for I cannot bear that you should hate him.

Though this may have been said before in my writings, and may be said again, the student who has not discovered this great compassion that William Shakespeare had for erring human nature, which is found in all his serious work, has missed the meaning of the plays completely, no matter how scholarly he may be or how deeply steeped in the lore of the ages. In this play, may we repeat, Shakespeare emphasizes Macbeth's suffering more than he does his crimes. He shows us a man of deep convictions who was not a murderer at heart becoming not only a murderer but a butcher all through his first mistake. But it is not Macbeth's crimes that have kept the play alive through the centuries. If the play were only a story of a series of crimes, it would not be worth reading. If the hero were only a murderer, we would recoil from him, and Shakespeare never incites hatred for a character who has come to a tragic end through a fatal mistake resulting from human weakness.

The murder of the Macduff family can never be condoned or excused on any ground. The only explanation that can be offered is that Macbeth has become so much on the defensive that he is striking out wildly. Not only has he descended further on his criminal path, but his mental suffering has been increased so greatly that he is on the point of breaking. After the death of Duncan, the burden of his tortured thought was that his fears in Banquo stuck deep. On the night of Banquo's murder, he told his wife that his mind was full of scorpions. When he resolves on the death of Macduff, he tries to delude himself that with Macduff out of the way, he will be able to sleep in spite of thunder. This desperate, despairing, tortured need of sleep cannot be overestimated or overstated. In his wretched need for sleep, we realize his bondage to the monster, evil, that he has embraced. The only thing that saved him from an end similar to that of his wife was his belief in the promises of the Witches. Again we must generalize and say that the thought uppermost in Shakespeare's mind in writing this play was that once we begin trafficking with evil we are dealing with a gigantic, violent, uncontrollable force that eludes our puny grasp once we have set it in motion.

In the scene with the Witches, Act IV, Scene I, the most significant speech is found about line 100.

> Yet my heart
> Throbs to know one thing: tell me, if your art
> Can tell so much: shall Banquo's issue ever
> Reign in this Kingdom?

This has been his most tormenting thought from the beginning. It was his first reaction to the Witches' prophecy at their appearance. He grasped that prediction before he noted that they had promised him the crown. When Duncan was murdered, his deepest regret was that he had defiled his mind for the descendants of Banquo. In the beginning he was willing to commit murder in order to establish a dynasty, and this has been his keenest disappointment. Before the murder of Banquo he said, in soliloquy, that the Witches had placed a fruitless crown upon his head and a barren sceptre in his gripe, which would be wrenched from him by another family, or line, and no son of his would succeed to the throne. His "vaulting ambition" has not been for himself alone. Now, standing before the Witches with his mind full of scorpions, his heart throbs to know whether Banquo's family will ever reign in the kingdom.

The student who has watched Shakespeare's way of working for many years comes to have a certain sense of sureness about how much one is intended to believe of what any character is saying. In the case of Ross's report to Macduff and Malcolm, describing conditions in Scotland, I feel sure we are expected to accept it on the whole as a picture of a devastated land. At the same time we somehow know we are to remember that evil once set in motion rages far beyond the control of the one who loosed it upon the world, and we find ourselves thinking, or knowing, that Macbeth's agents carried on the work he had begun while Macbeth himself had little knowledge of what they were doing. This, however, does not absolve him to any extent from responsibility, but it does soften the picture many students have of Macbeth storming rampant about the country.

It is a defiant Macbeth whom we find at the beginning of Act V, Scene III. He has gone to Dunsinane Hill where he is counting on the two prophecies of the Witches; (1) that no man born of woman shall have power over him; (2) that he will not be vanquished until Birnam Wood shall come to Dunsinane. He now says that his false thanes, like Macduff, may fly to England and enjoy the luxurious life they will find there. For himself—the mind by which he directs his course will never sag with doubt, and the heart he bears in his breast will never shake with fear. No, he needs fear nothing till Birnam Wood shall come to Dunsinane, and that possibility is absurd. And, after all, what is the boy Malcolm? Was he not born of woman? This defiance does not sound altogether like bravado. Rather, it appears to be a momentary resurgence of the great courage that was once his strongest characteristic.

As he reflects upon these things, there comes a message with the news that a British force of ten thousand men is moving against him. Immediately he is sick at heart and says that the approaching battle will either result in a happy life or will dethrone him. But he knows in his heart that there is no hope for happiness. Suddenly he feels old and says with infinite sadness,

> I have lived long enough, my way of life
> Is fallen into the sear, the yellow leaf
> And that which should accompany old age,
> As honor, love, obedience, troops of friends,
> I must not look to have; but in their stead
> Curses, not loud but deep, mouth-honor, breath
> Which the poor heart would fain deny and dare not.

Here we find the dream that was his before the play began —a dream which pictured his declining years passed with troops of friends, enjoying the honors and privileges of a well-spent life. Instead of these things he had dreamed of, he now has only the verbal honors due to a king which he would like to disclaim but dare not.

When the news of the approaching army is confirmed, he has a spurt of physical courage and declares he will fight till the flesh is hacked from his bones, and he will hang any who talk of fear.

When the Doctor appears, the anguished plea which Macbeth makes to him seems like an agonized query which his tormented mind has made for himself and his wife many times. He asks if the Doctor cannot minister to a mind diseased, pluck from the memory a rooted sorrow, erase the engraven troubles of the brain and with some sweet, oblivious-bringing antidote, cleanse the overburdened bosom of the perilous grief that stifles the heart.

If this sketch were a study of the character of Lady Macbeth, the sleepwalking scene would call for careful analysis. A common misreading of Lady Macbeth's lines about her little hand appears to me important enough to deserve passing mention. It has been stated many times that Lady Macbeth was a small, dainty woman because of her reference to her little hand. To me that line has always meant that her hand was small in comparison with the great quantities of perfumes which, in Shakespeare's time, came pouring in from Arabia. I think of Lady Macbeth as a beautiful, perhaps stately, woman but not necessarily a small, delicate one.

From now on, except for the brief passages of defiance, the lines of Macbeth are so heavily weighted with sorrow and their poetry so poignantly beautiful and moving that one feels more diffident and inadequate than usual in attempting to comment on them. Nevertheless, a student who has been over the ground many times may venture to call attention to impressive passages and important meanings that might escape the notice of one who has been less frequently along the way. Sometimes it seems best to let the words of the nobler passages march on in their own majesty, not scrutinizing too carefully their detailed significance. Again, careful examination of the meanings which bring a better understanding of the lines may throw light on their poetic effect and further enhance their beauty.

When Macbeth hears the cry of the women he knows, without asking the occasion of their weeping, although he does not ask about the weeping until later. He is surprised that the news of his wife's death brings no shock to his nervous system. He has forgotten the taste of fears, he says. There had been a time when his senses would have frozen, and his smooth hair would have stood on end at hearing a dismal story, he adds. This terrible fear had begun on that night when Duncan was murdered, when the knocking at the gate made him ask himself, "How is it with me when every noise appalls me?" On that night she had been waiting for him at the bottom of the stairs with her stalwart support and loyal sympathy. "Why, worthy thane," she had said, "do you bend your noble strength to think so brainsickly of things?" After her own visit to the death chamber she was mortally shaken herself, and yet she took full command of the practical situation and, hurrying him to the bedroom lest they be found watching, she had a word of comfort for him as she urged him not to be lost so poorly in his thoughts. Now she is dead, and he has supped so full of horrors that the direst things cannot startle him, so familiar has he become with horrible evil and murderous thoughts.

When Seyton re-enters and tells him the Queen is dead, he says, with the deepest sadness, that she should have lived longer. Under ordinary conditions she would have had many years to live. Then there would have been time to speak of the word "death" and its meaning, also time for the expression of his own grief. This is my own interpretation of this speech. For years critics have found callous indifference in the line, "She should have died hereafter." Although quaintly phrased its meaning seems clear. It simply means that she should have died at some later time, or, still more simply, she should have lived longer. Yes, he continues, under normal conditions there would have been time for the expression of his own grief. But now she is gone, and the sun will come up tomorrow as the sun has come up on the day following the passing of the great and the humble, even as the sun came up on that day following the murder of Duncan without seeing his departure from Inverness, because the woman had willed it so. Another tomorrow will come and still another tomorrow, and the days will move slowly on in their petty pace to the last syllable of recorded time. How slowly the reader must say those words "Tomorrow, and tomorrow, and tomorrow!" to suggest slow creeping time! And all the yesterdays will be like candle-bearing servants going before their masters to their bedrooms, these beacon-like yesterdays lighting man's way to his last resting-place where his body will turn to dust. Perhaps in the line which follows, "Out, out, brief candle," he is admonishing his own brief candle to go out. Against this stupendous background of passing time Macbeth sees the individual life moving like a tiny, fleeting shadow, his little moment against this vast setting being like the role of a poor player who frets his little hour upon the stage and then is heard no more. A human life-story, he concludes, is like a rambling irresponsible tale told by an idiot in which there is only sound and madness, all of which signifies nothing.

Macbeth is the only one of Shakespeare's four giants who has this tremendous conception or vision of time—time running through the roughest day, time stretching out to the crack of doom and time creeping, creeping in its petty pace from day to day to the last syllable of its own record. Again may I say, at the risk of becoming tiresome, that it is inconceivable that anyone could believe that a man with this tremendous breadth of vision would of his own volition commit murder for a petty little personal ambition.

He is the only one of the four giants who has committed unspeakable crimes, and yet whom Shakespeare defies us to call a criminal. And Shakespeare has given him the most glorious imagination of them all.

When the news of the moving wood comes to him, Macbeth is characteristically defiant, and he then decides to move out of the castle which, at the beginning of the scene he had declared to be impregnable. Militarily this is said to have been a great mistake, and the move gives further proof of his tendency to panic. Outside he finds himself in the position of a bear tied to a stake, but still declares his intention of putting up a fight. He has one last hope in the prophecy that no man born of woman shall ever slay him. He fights for a moment with young Siward, slays him and then Macduff comes on the scene. Macbeth is alone and has been debating in his own mind the advisability of dying on his own sword as many an ancient Roman had done. He has become a-weary of the world, he has said a moment ago, but decides that the gashes his sword can make will do better on the enemy than on himself. When Macduff commands him to turn and face him, he expresses the deepest remorse. He does not wish to add to the great injury he has already done to the man before him—a deed that has further blackened and defiled his soul. His remorse is genuine. When he is informed that Macduff was not born in the normal way, he curses the Witches for their prophecy but declares he will not fight Macduff. Yet neither will he yield to kiss the ground before the feet of young Malcolm—whose appointment furnished the first step on his downward path. And he will not be tormented by the curses of the rabble. So, even though all the prophecies have failed, he will try for his last chance and will fight it out in personal combat.

Two of Shakespeare's four giants are soldiers. In his last moments Othello's thoughts turn to the services he has done for the state, and he struts for one proud moment across the stage before taking his own life. Macbeth has forgotten his military glory and his services to the state. There is no flash of memory bringing regrets for the "pride, pomp and circumstance of glorious war" (though Macbeth probably had not known that kind of war). A lifetime of suffering has come between his military life and the present. Now he is thinking only of the wrong he has done to the man before him. (The real criminal is a man without a conscience.) He recovers his personal courage, the note on which the play began, and, finding the fight inevitable, goes out with a challenging cry that rings in the ears of the meditative student for a long time— "Lay on Macduff!" Soon after these words are spoken Macduff, following the custom of the times, brings the head of Macbeth and lays it at the feet of Malcolm. The nobles rejoice and hail Malcolm King of Scotland. The hideous reign of terror is at an end, and Scotland is once more free.

But the student who has lived with this play until the leaves of the book have become soft with much turning may find himself thinking back over the life of this ill-fated man who had been persuaded into committing a crime that was abhorrent to him from its inception, pushed into something that scarred his soul and rendered him incapable of carrying out the plan even in the exalted position where his actions were in no danger of being challenged. As this student recalls the agonizing sleepless nights and dwells for a moment on the mind full of scorpions, he may find himself thinking of Macbeth's own words and saying with a sigh of relief, "Macbeth is in his grave. After life's fitful fever he sleeps well."

OTHELLO

SHAKESPEARE sometimes begins a play, or a scene, in the middle of a conversation. What has gone before is soon revealed, and the play suffers no loss. In fact, the unusualness of the unfoldment often adds a certain flavor of interest to the exposition. In this play, however, the slight reversal of their presentation has often led to a misinterpretation of the events and of their relative importance.

The facts are these. Before the play opens Roderigo, who is a dissolute aristocrat, has sought the hand of Desdemona in marriage, and has been vehemently rebuffed by her father. Iago has built up Roderigo's hopes by promising him that Desdemona's favor can be bought with gifts of jewelry. Iago has pretended to buy these intercessory jewels with Roderigo's money. Iago has no intention of carrying out his part of the bargain, a filthy bargain which, failing to win Desdemona as Roderigo's wife, will give him access to her bedroom. Then Roderigo learns that Desdemona has been married to the Moor, Othello, and he develops an intense hatred for Othello. As the scene opens Roderigo is violently upbraiding Iago for having knowledge of the approaching marriage while still accepting his money. Iago has learned that the way to get along with Roderigo is to agree with him whenever possible, and it is very necessary at this time to keep in the good graces of Roderigo in order to retain hold on his purse strings. So he pretends that he, too, hates Othello. With diabolical cleverness and incredible alacrity, he trumps up the story about Cassio's promotion and his own repudiation by Othello. But it must be noted, and kept in mind, that originally it was Roderigo who hated Othello. Interwoven in Iago's story and only partially disguised is the revelation of his own real hatred, a smouldering hostility toward and envy of Michael Cassio. When Edwin Booth, at the opening of the play, sat glaring at Othello with those large, luminous eyes of his blazing hatred, it must have made tremendous acting, but I suspect that he, along with many others, may have missed the entire meaning of the play. At least a problem confronting the careful reader is to discover just how much Iago does hate Othello, at least in the beginning, and how much Othello has become entangled in Iago's hatred for Cassio.

The story that Iago tells Roderigo about the promotion of Cassio over him is not true, although it has been accepted by many discriminating scholars. Careless reading alone can account for this misapprehension, careless reading which for the moment dulls their alertness to one of the most essential requirements of Shakespearean character analysis. That requirement is that the reader must never accept, or must always be ready to challenge, the word of any character unless the veracity of that character has been established, or unless the statement is accepted by more than one person of confirmed honesty.

Time was in the early history of the drama when the people of the play did not speak as individuals. They came on the stage one after another and, in a sprightly manner, told a story, each contributing a part. Gradually the playwrights began having the players express their own opinions or thoughts. More and more they came to speak "in character." By the time Shakespeare began writing, character delineation was approaching the peak of its development and, under the pen of William Shakespeare the players appeared as real people, standing on their own feet and being responsible for their own acts and their own words. Philosophers and dupes appeared, lovers had their little hour upon the stage, and liars and deceivers plied their schemes and machinations surreptitiously or unabashed. Therefore, every line of Shakespeare must be examined as to its truthfulness, with the requirements mentioned applied as tests: namely, is the statement given by a person of known trustworthiness, and is it accepted by more than one person of discrimination and veracity (one person might be deceived as was Othello)?

One can point to five or more reasons for the conclusion that Iago is lying.

First——In the very opening lines of the play, Iago is presented to us as having his hand in another man's purse. The two men are alone, and when Roderigo makes the accusation Iago does not deny it. In fact, he verifies it by further demands for money. Now a man who has his hand in another man's pocket is demonstrably a thief and in all probability a liar.

Second——The matter of Cassio's promotion is never mentioned again in the play. It is not told to any responsible person. The story is told only to the dupe whom Iago wishes to impress with his own importance. Incidentally the "three great ones" are not identified. If they really existed, would not Iago have flaunted their names before Roderigo? If Iago had been as badly disappointed as he pretends to be, would he not have harped on it, more or less, throughout the play? And would not others have mentioned it? Emilia never refers to Iago's disappointment and continues to address Cassio as "my good lieutenant."

Third——Would not Othello have appointed Iago immediately to the lieutenancy if he had been Cassio's equal or superior? Why does Othello leave the lieutenancy vacant unless he had some unexpressed intention of restoring Cassio to his former rank when he thinks he has had sufficient discipline and when the official whom Cassio had offended has been placated or the offense had time to cool?

Fourth——Othello does not appoint Iago to the lieutenancy until Iago has worn him down to agonizing suspicion and until Othello kneels in great anguish, vowing revenge. Then Iago kneels beside him, hypocritically asking the stars and all the earthly elements to witness his vow to give all his powers to Othello's service. Then, and not until then, does Othello say, "Now art thou my lieutenant." This is not the well-weighed decision of a military man, but the emotional response of a greatly distraught mind to what appears to be genuine sympathy.

Fifth——Why does the Senate at Venice appoint Cassio to succeed Othello as Governor of Cyprus (toward the close of the play) if they did not consider him closely equal to Othello in all respects? It should be recalled that they were discriminating enough to choose Othello as their military leader in spite of his race.

The crowning reason for Iago's lie must be left until later in the discussion. Shakespeare was a master of keeping suspense, but in this particular play one wishes he could blurt out the reasons for Iago's antagonism toward Cassio. The explanation comes so late in the play and is missed by so many students because it is brought in with a rush of concluding events. Shakespeare was patient enough to develop a character slowly.

Other significant points to be considered in this connection are: Iago's underhanded, dishonorable, scheming relationship with Roderigo, the most disreputable person in the play, would in itself argue against his being officer material. He is known as "honest Iago," a reputation he doubtless built up for himself, because a person whose trustworthiness is above question is not usually referred to as being honest. No one in the play speaks of "honest Othello" or "honest Desdemona." Their honesty is taken for granted. Iago's appellation for himself was repeated inadvertently by others in the play and, unfortunately, has been accepted by many otherwise discriminating scholars. Outstanding among their number, we find the once highly esteemed and now deeply revered George Lyman Kittredge, of Harvard, who accepted Iago's story in its entirety. Can one imagine the Iago of Dr. Kittredge whose "military record is unassailable" who is "actuated by resentment of injustice" stooping to the unsavory association with Roderigo and treacherously plotting the pitfall into which Cassio unsuspectingly falls? Can one imagine a man of officer material with his warped and corrupt ideas of morals? How could the fine upstanding officer of the brilliant misreaders of the play have degenerated into a foulmouthed, evil-minded liar merely because of a military disappointment no matter how crushing the impact of that disappointment? And, incidentally, where in the play does one find the "unassailable military record," mentioned by Kittredge, except in Iago's own words?

Dr. Frank C. Baxter, the brilliant lecturer, who through the medium of television has brought Shakespeare into many homes and thereby enriched the lives of many people in America, must be numbered among that naive, trusting group who accept the cock-and-bull story that Iago tells to Roderigo.

When such old time critics as H. N. Hudson, who wrote nearly a hundred years ago, saw that Iago was not acting from revenge, one is more than surprised to find modern critics, who have had the advantage of the progress that has been made in the study of abnormal psychology, accepting Iago for anything but what he is, and what Shakespeare intended him to be—a psychopathic personality. But more of that later. When Shakespeare puts into the mouth of Iago such offensive lines as the one about the black ram and the white ewe, those revolting lines are not mere smut intended for the ears of the groundlings. They are strong character lines indicating the habitual trend of Iago's thoughts.

The last word on the subject, as on all Shakespearean tragedy, must come from A. C. Bradley who says, "One must constantly remember not to believe a syllable that Iago utters on any subject, including himself, until one has tested his statement by comparing it with known facts and with other statements of his own or of other people, and by considering whether he had in the particular circumstances any reason for telling a lie or for telling the truth. The implicit confidence which his acquaintances placed in his integrity has descended to most of his critics, and this, reinforced by the comical habit of quoting as Shakespeare's own statement anything said by his characters, has been a fruitful source of misinterpretation, . . . if there is any fact at all behind Iago's account of the conversation (of Othello and the three great ones), it doubtless is the fact that Iago himself was ignorant of military science while Cassio was an expert, and that Othello explained this to the great personages. That Cassio, again, was an interloper and a mere closet student is incredible considering that Othello chose him for his lieutenant, and secondly, that the Senate appointed him to succeed Othello in command at Cyprus." [1]

In the first scene, Roderigo has referred to Othello as "thick lips." No other character in the play attributes any such negroid features to Othello, and it should be remembered that Roderigo has a half-insane prejudice against and hatred for Othello. Brabantio refers to his "sooty bosom," but may he not have meant his hairy chest? Some rather fair men have black hair on their chests. The word "sooty" seems to apply more aptly to this interpretation than it does to a mere black body. All other characters refer to Othello respectfully as "the Moor" or "the valiant Moor." It is only Iago who brings out the racial comparison when he refers to Othello as a black ram and Desdemona as a white ewe. Is it not possible that the foul-mouthed Iago's obscene description has been taken too seriously?

[1] A. C. Bradley. *Shakespearean Tragedy*, pages 211-212.

It is certain that Shakespeare never knew the American ne-gro. Shakespeare died in 1616, and the first American coloni-zations began in 1607 and 1620. It was some time after this latter date that the importations of slaves from the jungles of Africa to America began. Shakespeare may have had some hearsay knowledge of negroes in the wilds of Africa, from the tales of explorers, but he really knew only the black men of northern Africa who had lived along the shores of the Mediterranean and who for many centuries had been in con-tact with white civilization. When we think of the advances which the American negro, or mulatto, has made in less than four centuries, we may realize the degree of culture and civ-ilization that had been attained by the dark races of the Med-iterranean lands. Most, or many, of them had some white blood with the abilities and ambitions of the white race. Some of them had dark skin and Caucasian features. This is no place to go into a study of the Moors as a race of people. That in-formation can be found in any good encyclopedia.

Then, since it is only the violently prejudiced Roderigo who called Othello "thick lips," surely we may place a ques-tion mark after the malicious epithet. In Shakespeare's time people of dark complexion were often called "black." In the Elizabethan age the English were a fairer people than they are today, and brunets were possibly as rare as natural blonds are in our time. True, Othello speaks of himself as being black, but Cleopatra also called herself black, and we do not think of her as a negress. In the Sonnets and in *Love's Labour's Lost*, black is constantly employed in the sense of dark complex-ioned. Othello was a Mauritanian prince. The Venetians had nothing to do with negroes, but they had much intercourse with the Moors, who were a civilized, warlike, enterprising race, such as might well furnish an Othello.[1]

In Act I, Scene III, the "valiant Othello," as the Duke calls him, comes into the august presence of the Venetian Senators.

[1] Summarized from Hudson.

He enters with others but can be singled out by his soldierly bearing in which there appears a certain pride in his calling but no petty self-confidence. His appearance is that of a man mellowed more by experience than by years. He is not handsome as to facial features but has a good physique. When he stands to speak it is with a simple dignity and natural nobility. The deep organ tones of his resonant voice, the rich quality of which was born to him in a southern climate, commands the spellbound attention of his audience. His speech has nothing of the hangdog confession about it. It is a straightforward narrative given with a rare mingling of self-possession and gentleness. As he delivers his captivating summary of the story that is the history of his life, we are struck with the thought that Desdemona, despite her innocence and modesty, may have made the first advances in their love-making. In fact, he goes on to say that she bade him, if he had a friend that loved her he should but teach him how to tell his story, and that would woo her. Later, listening to Iago's ribald account of Venetian women, the memory of those maidenly advances would return to plague him with doubts.

Desdemona does not speak to her father with youthful defiance, but with a dignified earnestness that all but matches the Moor's solemn declaration, as she tells how she has consecrated her soul to his fortunes.

The Senate scene should be studied carefully in order to reach an adequate appreciation of the frankly declared love of these newly wedded people. Only by realizing the great depth of their love can one grasp the enormity of Iago's hideous crime against them. Some of the commentators tell us that it was a love in which one great soul called to another, but each reader must find his own evidence of such a love in the lines of the play. Careful study will convince him that theirs was a greater, deeper love than the impetuous love of Romeo and Juliet or the impassioned love of Antony and Cleopatra. These last named plays are regarded as Shakespeare's greatest love stories. This is true because in those plays the tragedy evolves out of the love-story itself. In this play the lovers are the victims of an outside force, and that outside force furnishes the conflict which is necessary to every dramatic plot.

From their respective accounts of their courtship we may draw our own picture, inadequate but suggestive. It is a picture of a girl listening wide-eyed to a man's descriptions of places and experiences that she never had heard of. Interest turned into pity as he told of the many hardships that had come to him. As the musical voice rolled on many a poetic phrase came from the speaker's lips, delighting and fascinating the girl who listened. His remarkable poise and self-possession began to attract her attention, and beyond all these things she recognized a great soul. So it was that Othello came to tower far above the curled darlings of her own city and generation with their limited experiences and their trivial conversations. On Othello's part, his occasional polite glances in the direction of the girl became a thoughtful attention as he began to see her sympathetic responses to his stories. Then her starry-eyed recognition of him as a man caused a strange awakening of something long dormant within him, and behind the starry eyes he, too, found a beautiful soul.

Having picked up the idea that he hates Othello (in his first conversation with Roderigo) Iago plays with the thought again in soliloquy at the close of Act I, Scene III. He gives the only reason for this pretended hatred that his profligate mind can conceive—a suspicion of Othello and Emilia. One may read that soliloquy over and over without finding a shred of evidence that he himself believes what he is saying about his hatred or about his suspicion of Othello and Emilia. The mere statement is made about the two, and it is not followed up by any expression of resentment or injured pride or outraged feelings such as would have been the reaction of any normal man. These spurious statements are made quite casu-

ally. It seems impossible that this hatred could have any substance without his revealing it in some way or to someone.
No one in the play ever gives the slightest hint of a suggestion that Iago has anything but the highest regard for Othello.
It is only to Roderigo and in soliloquy that he expresses this
hatred and gives his unsubstantial and unsubstantiated reasons
for doing so. Just how far he was able to goad himself into
something resembling hatred as the plot develops would be
difficult to determine. It is next to impossible to pin down the
pathological liar. (To digress for a moment, it seems unbelievable that Othello would have trusted his young wife to the
care of Emilia on the voyage to Cyprus, or that he would
have retained her as his wife's waiting-maid if she had ever
been his mistress or if there had ever been anything question-
able about their relations.)

Now Iago's mind is wholly occupied with his plan for the
undoing of Cassio. His purpose to ensnare Cassio will work
better because of Othello's approval of him (Iago), he reflects. He will be able to keep that approval more easily, perhaps, because he harbors no real hatred for Othello. So the
"monstrous birth" takes place, the birth of his plan to sow
seeds of suspicion in the mind of Othello concerning Cassio
and Desdemona. In this speech Iago has paid Cassio a distinct
compliment—though he turns the asset to a liability. He
speaks of Cassio's "smooth dispose" which means his agree-
able manners.[1] Cassio's fine manners are a source of annoy-
ance and envy to Iago throughout the play. Bradley says,
speaking of Iago, "Of his origin we are ignorant, but, unless
I am mistaken, he was not of gentle birth or breeding." [2]

The first scene of Act II may seem to the casual reader
merely an extension of the plot showing the three parties arriving at Cyprus, but a careful study finds the scene rich in

---

[1] See "smooth"—Random House College Dictionary; and "dispose" in
O.E.D. and *A Shakespeare Word Book* by John Foster.
[2] *Shakespearean Tragedy*, page 213.

character lines. It is almost as if Shakespeare were saying, You have met most of these people before, but I have gathered them together here where they will have the opportunity of speaking for themselves informally but in character.

Cassio is introduced first. We have had only a glimpse of him in Act I. Before he comes on the scene we are told that he "looks sadly, and prays the Moor be safe." When Cassio makes his appearance it is with a prayer on his lips that the heavens give Othello defense against the elements. He closes his speech by saying, "*I have lost him on a dangerous sea.*" An accident to Othello would have been felt first as a personal loss to himself. He describes Desdemona to Montano in glowing, enthusiastic terms which have no suggestion of personal interest in her. When he learns that Iago's ship has arrived (though it started later than his own and Othello's) he knows immediately that they have escaped the storms encountered by the other ships. He picturesquely describes the tempest-tossed sea, giving up for the time-being its destructive nature in order that the "divine" Desdemona may go safely by. The word "divine" was often used in Shakespeare's time to mean "enjoying supreme felicity, happy, fortunate." Shakespeare used it in this sense in *Venus and Adonis*.[1] This interpretation of the word obviates the impression, which a cursory reading might give, that Cassio is expressing his own admiration for Desdemona. Then again Cassio prays that Jove will guard Othello so that he will soon be in Desdemona's arms, and bring comfort to the quenched or dampened spirits of the group. This great loyalty to and affection for Othello prepares us for the stunning blow he receives when Othello dismisses him.

In a casual reading of *Othello*, it may seem that the character of Cassio is not sufficiently well drawn, because, for reasons connected with his portrayal of Iago, Shakespeare delays the full characterization of Cassio until almost the end

[1] See "devine" O.E.D.

of the play. However, we have a number of brief revelations of his personality that mark him distinctly—in his genuine anxiety for Othello's safety, in his abstaining from taking part in the bold and suggestive comments of Iago to the two women as they wait for Othello's ship and, a little later, in his sincere regret about the loss of his reputation after he has partaken of the wine which Iago has forced upon him. The final full revelation of the character of Cassio may come like a bombshell even to the careful reader. It opens up the entire pattern of the play, revealing in a sudden flash the cause of Iago's malignity and his antagonism to Cassio. How wise Shakespeare was to have withheld this vital information until Iago himself reveals it. Thus he rounds out perfectly the abnormal character he is portraying, the person who admits the truth only when he is finally driven into a corner. All this will be fully considered later.

In connection with the conversation between Cassio and Montano, it should be noted that there is no question or word of disapproval of the marriage of Desdemona and the Moor. The union seems to meet his heartiest endorsement. In fact Brabantio and Roderigo are the only ones in the play who censure or condemn the marriage.

It is in this scene (Act II, Scene I) where we first see the newly wedded couple together in an exchange of conversation. They have both appeared before the Senate, but have spoken separately. At first sight of Desdemona, Othello calls out, "O, my fair warrior!" Then, as he comes closer, he says with deep emotion, "O, my soul's joy!" Shakespeare can tell volumes in a few words. In all his serious work we find short sentences which sometimes tell the whole story of the tragedy. In *Hamlet* the five words, "Frailty, thy name is woman," tell the moving story of a disillusioned youth. Romeo's "O, I am Fortune's fool!" reveals the plight of the star-crossed lovers, and Coriolanus' "There is a world elsewhere" speaks volumes of that hero's determination. Each of these sentences has five words. Othello's four words, "O, my soul's joy," tell us that this beautiful Venetian girl has brought great joy, felicity, bliss to the very depths of his soul. This exquisitely beautiful love that has come to a thoughtful, earnest man is indescribably impressive. For him it is heaven on earth. And all the while, almost within arm's length, stands Iago, the embodiment of evil, like the serpent in the Garden of Eden. Othello continues to say that his soul feels such absolute contentment in this reunion that he is sure he will never again know such complete and perfect happiness. Thus, like a cloud floating across a summer sky, Shakespeare gives us a foreshadowing of what is to come.

Desdemona's reply to Othello is in the same vein as his own as she prays that their love and comforts (support and encouragement) shall increase, giving each other moral and physical strength as their lives continue. (Shakespeare's once rich words must sometimes be supplemented today by synonyms and connotations.)

This is the first time we have met Iago in any other company than that of Roderigo. His coarse remarks about women are accepted by Desdemona as small talk or harmless jesting (while all the time she is watching for Othello's ship), but Cassio comments to Desdemona that Iago speaks too bluntly, and she must take him as a soldier, not as a scholar. Iago knows his own manners are not those of a gentleman and, watching Cassio and Desdemona, he sees, or pretends to see, lechery in their friendly holding of hands. Even Roderigo, rogue that he is, was reared in gentility and sees only courtesy in Cassio's courtly manners, which Iago resents.

So by the end of Scene I, Act II, we have a fairly comprehensive understanding of the vicious, depraved mind of Iago and of his diabolical plan, as yet not completely unfolded, for the undoing of Michael Cassio. Iago has placed his unholy hand upon the wheel of Fortune, and into its resultant monstrous grinding the lives of Othello and Desdemona will be enmeshed. But, it will be found, and it is most important to note, that Othello does not respond to Iago's subtle insinuations and later bold accusations in the way that Iago counted on. Iago expected Othello to be so overcome with uncontrollable anger that he would wreak some horrible, appalling vengeance on Cassio. While Othello does order the execution of Cassio in the midst of the final turmoil, his thoughts have turned from the very first to Desdemona and what he thinks is her unbelievable defection. So, Iago has met his first defeat in the very workings of Othello's upright mind.

Iago is not a villain in the commonly accepted sense of the term, although that is the label usually attached to him. To quote from Hazelton Spencer,[1] "Back of the Shakespearean villain lay centuries of stage-villainy: there was the Devil of the medieval mystery plays; there was Judas, most incomprehensible of villains; there were the bad angels of the morality plays—no motivation was needed for them; there was the Vice of the later moralities and interludes, the mischief-making mainspring of every plot, who neither required nor received any accounting for; and there were the sinister Italian scoundrels of more recent drama, men with the weasel words of Machiavelli on their lips, as the Tudor age misunderstood Machiavelli, or desperate Dons, like Lorenzo in *The Spanish Tragedie*, whose wicked designs are scarcely motivated at all. For an audience habituated to the machinations of a villain as essential to the plot of a serious play, a study of the cause of his anti-social conduct was as little called for as a rehearsal of the reasons why a hero was a normal man or a good man. All the dramatist had to do was to exhibit his hero and villain; the audience did the rest."

Those of us who belong to that school of thought which believes that Shakespeare's characters may be studied as real people and not merely as actors on the Elizabethan stage, bound by the limitations of Elizabethan thought, are inclined

[1] *The Art and Life of William Shakespeare*, pages 321-322.

to follow Shakespeare, in our minds, away from the theatre and into his study where we think we can come closer to his conception of the characters he created there. That Shakespeare was keenly interested in the study of the abnormal mind is commonly accepted among students. Opportunities for such study were at hand in real life and in books. In the printing shop of Richard Fields (a Stratford boy about Shakespeare's age, who went to London a short time before Shakespeare did), there was a book called *A Treatice of Melancholy* written by Timothy Bright.[1] "Melancholy," in those days, covered the general ground of gloominess, irascibility, sullenness, despondency, hypochondria, morbidity, frenzy, and madness. (This list is from Hardin Craig.) It has been reasonably supposed that Shakespeare frequented this print shop and became familiar with this book. It would serve as a foundation study of abnormal psychology, which would be pursued in many directions by the natural psychologist which we know Shakespeare to have been. Shakespeare's time had seen a radical change in the attitude of the intelligent public toward unstable and insane people. Previously they had been treated as criminals or as objects of ridicule. There was no sympathetic understanding of their condition or their needs. With greater enlightenment these unfortunates became the objects of more compassionate consideration, and Shakespeare found in them an ever-increasing interest. Iago is his most outstanding and obvious presentation of a maladjusted person.

Perhaps it should be mentioned here that Shakespeare had no knowledge of the terminology used in present-day psychology. One may look in vain, for example, in a Shakespeare Concordance for the word "emotion," and it will seem strange, since the dramatist described the whole gamut of

[1] A facsimile of this book has been printed recently by Columbia University Press with Introduction by Hardin Craig in which mention is made of a number of other works on "melancholy," which may have been available to Shakespeare.

human emotions. Nor is it likely that Shakespeare had any extended acquaintance with the causes of abnormal behavior. Unfavorable childhood experiences which, we know today, result in instability of character had not been traced to their unhappy development by him or his contemporaries. Therefore, there is no reference to the causes of Iago's villainy.

The suggestion that Iago may have been intentionally drawn as a psychopathic personality is not new. Some of the commentators have skirted around the subject without really committing themselves to a definite theory. Even a casual scrutiny of a book on case histories of psychopathic patients will find Iago peeping out from many of its pages. Still more, Iago's name will be found appearing occasionally in bold print in books on abnormal psychology. Different names are used to designate different types of abnormal persons, yet no agreement as to exact terms has ever been reached by scientists. A person may be abnormal or unstable in so many varying degrees that a very large list of names would be required for the many differing types. The term "psychopathic personality" or "psychopath" is the one most generally and perhaps loosely used to describe people who are not normal and yet are not definitely psychotic.

In recent years some of the terminology used by the psychologist and the psychiatrist has crept into the conversation of the layman who, all too often, uses them with little discriminating understanding of their proper meaning. Frequently such words as "psychopath" or "neurotic" are used to describe a person whom the speaker dislikes or with whom he disagrees. So a somewhat more accurate conception of "psychopathic personality" must be suggested here (even though most unprofessional). The material is culled from here and there among books on abnormal psychology.

The psychopath is classed as sane and is supposedly responsible for his conduct, but he is not a normal person, and it is difficult to hold him responsible for his misdeeds. When sent to a mental hospital or caught in the meshes of the law, he manages to prove himself sane and is released. Usually he is attractive and clever and makes a good impression. He shows a total disregard for truth and has little or no sense of responsibility. Often he is very eloquent and convincing in speaking of his honor as a gentleman, but he has no conception of honor, no intention of living up to his word and is not embarrassed when confronted with his inconsistencies. He has no sense of shame and never shows any signs of regret. His distinguishing quality is egocentricity or self-centeredness. He has a most abnormal deadness of human feeling. He often holds a grudging spite against the goodness of men. The psychopath has no capacity for seeing himself as others see him and does not realize that he differs from other men. In a sense he is not a complete man but a robot. The affective side of his nature is entirely wanting but, robot-like, he can mimic the complete personality perfectly. He has no awareness of the meaningful aspects of life.

His reasoning takes the form of rationalization from which truth is entirely missing. If he commits a crime, he is incapable of pity, horror, mercy, or any of the emotional feelings that restrain a normal man. He is often antagonistic, especially to his superiors or any important person in his environment, and is capable of intense hatreds. Often he is found striving desperately to prevent others finding a full expression of their lives. In spite of all this, he often acquires a kind of culture and may be socially quite charming. He may have a large personal following, and his friends find it hard to believe when delinquency appears. A distinct feeling of inferiority is one of the outstanding characteristics of the psychopath. He uses many devices to conceal this feeling of inadequacy, and it is bafflingly interwoven with his egocentricity. He is a coward. He has an obscene mind. He has an almost uncanny cleverness at manipulating bits of knowledge in a way to make himself appear well-informed or even learned. He is unbelievably inconsistent. He will brazenly deny something he said in all earnestness only yesterday. He will reverse a stand he has taken on a controversial issue and do it in such a way as to defy anyone to contradict him or even remind him of his former opinions. He is always a vain man and, as Alfred Adler tells us,[1] "Vanity and the feeling for one's fellow man are not conceivable together. These two character traits can never be joined because vanity will not allow itself to be subordinated to the rules of society. . . . Vanity finds its fate within itself." Often the psychopath has one particular person in his life whom he secretly admires and at the same time envies. The expression of this envy can vary from a mild, half-humorous desire to humiliate or belittle the envied one to an all-absorbing wish to destroy him. When the envy is of the latter violent nature it will often run its course, and, strangely, when the abnormal one is cornered, he will blurt out the truth, revealing the causes of his envy and his enmity. We shall see how this applies to Iago.

There is a rule, if it may be called a rule, concerning character delineation which we learned from Clayton Hamilton[2] some years ago. The rule (given from memory) is that a character is convincing only if it is typical, and it is interesting only if it is individual. A character may be convincing as a representative of a class or group, but unless it has individuality it is not interesting. Or, a character may have abundant individuality and be interesting because of that feature, but unless it is typical of a class or group it is not convincing. In the foregoing discussion of the outstanding qualities of the psychopathic personality, we find Iago conforming, in the main, to a class—the class commonly called psychopaths. We discover also in studying his character that he has striking individual qualities, and so we find him interesting as a character even though we thoroughly dislike him as a person. So

[1] In *Understanding Human Nature.*
[2] *The Materials and Methods of Fiction.*

we must grant that Shakespeare has given us a striking character drawing in Iago, one far more convincing and interesting and tremendously more effective than the traditional villain.

But we must speak more specifically of one phase of Iago's abnormality. He has calculatingly built up a reputation for unassailable honor which others in the play call honesty. "Honesty," in Shakespeare's day, was a stronger word than it is today, and embraced a man's whole character. The false front was so convincing that it would have been a brave person who would have dared to challenge it. If Emilia had been astute enough to see through her husband and had dared to say that he was not honest, her word would not have been accepted by anyone. However, in her later use of the word "wayward" in connection with Iago, she may be showing more understanding than modern usage of the word might indicate. The word as we use it means little more than willful. Formerly it meant, "disposed to go counter to the wishes of others or to what is reasonable, conforming to no fixed rule or principle of conduct; erratic." [1] It is impossible to exaggerate the importance of this impregnable wall of incorruptible uprightness, which becomes the most powerful force in the play. And it is this false front of character-perfection against which Othello is broken even more than by the lying insinuations and machinations of a diabolically clever schemer. And this putting on of a convincing personality that goes unquestioned is one of the cleverest tricks of the psychopath. Given a person who is defenseless because of a "free and open nature," as was Othello, the deception becomes unspeakably cruel. Also, the egocentric is constantly striving to build up his prestige. Aside from the natural desire for money which every man may have, Iago's main purpose in demanding money from Roderigo was to build up his own prestige.

[1] See O.E.D.

A few of the Shakespearean critics have glimpsed Iago as an abnormal person. Only a few can be quoted. Some points from Bradley's illuminating character analysis must be given, although they do inadequate justice to the whole. "His creed . . . is that absolute egoism is the only rational and proper attitude, and that conscience and honor or any kind of regard for others is an absurdity. . . . When we meet him he is destitute of humanity, of sympathetic or social feeling. He shows no trace of affection and in the presence of the most terrible suffering he shows either pleasure or indifference, which if not complete is nearly so. . . . Whatever disturbs his sense of superiority irritates him at once. . . . What vestige of passion unsatisfied or passion gratified is visible in Iago? None: That is the very horror of him." [1] Bradley continues to say: "Resentment of Cassio's appointment is expressed in the first conversation with Roderigo, and from that moment it is never once mentioned again in the whole play. Hatred of Othello is expressed in the First Act alone. Desire to get Cassio's place scarcely appears after the first soliloquy, and when it is gratified Iago does not refer to it by a single word. The suspicion of Cassio's intrigue with Emilia emerges suddenly, as an afterthought, not in the first soliloquy but in the second and then disappears forever. Iago's 'love' for Desdemona is alluded to in the second soliloquy; there is not the faintest trace of it in word or deed either before or after. The mention of jealousy of Othello is followed by declarations that Othello is infatuated about Desdemona and is of a constant nature, and during Othello's sufferings Iago never shows a sign of the idea that he is now paying his rival in his own coin. In the second soliloquy he declares that he quite believes Cassio to be in love with Desdemona; it is obvious that he believes no such thing, for he never alludes to the idea again, and within a few hours describes Cassio in soliloquy as an honest

[1] Bradley. Pages 219-224.

fool. His final reason for ill will to Cassio never appears till the Fifth Act."

We find many words and phrases familiar to the student of abnormal psychology used in Bradley's analysis: "obscene mind," "deadness of feeling," "sense of superiority," "contempt of others," "longing to satisfy his sense of power," "astonishingly clever," etc.

Thomas Marc Parrott says, "The term 'honest' in Shakespeare's day carried a different implication from that it bears in our commercial age; it meant four-square, upright, and trustworthy. The trust reposed in Iago by all who knew him, even by his shrewd and worldly wife, shows how well he had imposed his mask upon the world." [1]

Richard Flatter's book, *The Moor of Venice*, has so much that is new and worth while that one is at a loss to find any short quotable lines. We can only recommend the reading of the book. However, this much may be added to our collection: "We have, I think, to dismiss the idea of Iago's activities being prompted by his yearning for military advancement. And I feel equally sure that we must dismiss the idea of an Iago seeking to avenge an act of adultery of which not even himself is convinced. Now if those two motives disappear, or are so insignificant that they dissolve in the main stream of the action, is there anything else that might serve as explanation of Iago's feelings toward Othello? . . . Here I have reached the point where I have to submit my contention, and this is, that Iago never—neither at the beginning of the play nor at any time during it—really hates his victim. He hates him as little as the cat hates the mouse with which it plays, or the boy hates the frog on which he makes his cruel experiments. And yet, there is one driving power in Iago, one single irresistible and uncontrollable impulse: his passion for play-

[1] Introduction to *Othello* in *Shakespeare, Twenty-three Plays and the Sonnets.*

acting. Once begun there is no holding him. To this passion
which he cannot suppress, he sacrifices everything. . . . My
suggestion, if accepted, would clear up the mysterious point
in Iago's psychology of which Bradley, it is evident, is so fully
aware. While agreeing on the one hand that Iago shows neither any passionate desire for advancement nor any passion
of hatred for Othello, I have on the other hand submitted that
there is indeed one passion in him, a passion so overwhelm-
ingly powerful that it leads irresistibly to action: his craze for
play-acting. . . . The solution of this puzzle (obviously a
case of dual personality) lies, I should say, in the fact that
Iago is an actor, one of those ingenious actors who have the
gift of persuading not only their public but themselves. . . .
How can we explain a mentality so contradictory in itself?
We can do so only in the way already suggested: it is the mentality of a crazy actor." [1]

Turning to the scientist we find Hervey Cleckley, in his
book, *The Mask of Sanity, An Attempt to Reinterpret the
So-called Psychopathic Personality*, writing of "Fictional
Characters Showing Personality Anomalies." He says in
part, "It is difficult to find in literature a character that could
be grouped with the cases studied here. Creative artists have
presented the villain, the psychotic, the psychoneurotic, the
erratic genius, the weak, the strong, the wise and the stupid;
but we seldom find in imaginative writing anyone who can
fit the picture which emerges as we consider the histories in
this volume. Often, however, we find characters who in
some aspect or in some phase of their activities suggest what
we have seen in the psychopath; . . . Iago, perhaps the most
interesting and ingenious creation of vindictiveness known to
man, carries out his schemes of hate and treachery without
adequate motivation in the ordinary sense."

Returning to the text, we find that by the end of Scene

[1] *The Moor of Venice*, Chapter VII.

III, Act II, Iago has Cassio "on the hip" and is ready to throw him. "On the hip" is a wrestling term meaning that a wrestler has his opponent in a position from which he can fling him to the ground. But before Iago has begun the execution of his plot Shakespeare pauses for a brief moment to give us a little gem of character delineation—a study in character contrast. It is the brief conversation between Cassio and Iago, at the beginning of Scene III, Act II, where they are speaking of Desdemona. Men often reveal themselves more than they know, or intend, in their conversations about women. In these few lines we find the coarseness of Iago and the refinement of Cassio. It was Shakespeare's last opportunity to make such a character comparison. This conversation, though seemingly unimportant, throws light on the most important question of the play and should not be regarded lightly.

Before deciding that Cassio was weak in yielding to Iago's persuasion to join in drinking to the health of Othello, we must notice his courteous and genuine wish to join in the toast to his general and his conscientious realization that he has taken too much. He begs the company not to think he is drunk and goes out. Entrances and exits often have great significance in Shakespeare and should always be watched carefully. As soon as Cassio fully realizes his condition, he makes his exit. We may reasonably suppose that he intends to go home and sleep off the effects of the drink, leaving the guard duty to Iago. We recall that he has just said to Othello that Iago has had instructions as to the duties of the guard.

Hudson's estimate of Cassio's character is worthy of consideration here. He says, "Cassio, all radiant as he is of truth and honor, makes a superb contrast to Iago. His nature is, I am apt to think, the finest grained and most delicately organized of all Shakespeare's men. . . . Iago can get no foul suggestion to stick upon him; everything of the sort just runs right off his mind, leaving it clean and sweet as ever. He cannot, indeed, resist the cup that brims and sparkles with good-fellowship; he is too polite and manly for that." [1]

Idealistic, or even sentimental, as some of these older critics, such as Hudson, just quoted, may appear, they often seem to have given more thought to Shakespeare's characters than many modern scholars. Dr. Frank C. Baxter, who introduced "Shakespeare on TV," finds Cassio a "mediocre" person. In reply to this I would ask three questions: (1) Would Iago have cared enough about a mediocre person to vent a terrible vindictiveness upon him? (2) Would so excellent and experienced a soldier as Othello have chosen a mediocre person to be his first assistant? (3) Would the veteran Senators of Venice, who (as has been pointed out earlier) were discriminating enough to choose the valiant Moor as their military leader, in spite of his color, have replaced him at the close of the play by a man of "mediocre" personality and ability? As has been said, or intimated in this sketch, the pinnacle position Cassio holds in the play is not disclosed until the very end.

But after his exit Cassio meets with Iago's "flock of drunkards" and is undone. Before we leave the scene of Cassio's disgrace, we must take special note of, and charge our memories with, his lament about the loss of his reputation. This poignant regret should not be taken to be mere drunken drivel. It is the anguished cry of a sobered man. It is serious enough and touching enough to make a deep impression even upon Iago. That lament will come echoing back to us later in a most surprising and fantastic way.

Othello does not dismiss Cassio for personal reasons or as a personal punishment. Cassio has struck one of the high officials of the city. Othello is responsible for the conduct of his soldiers toward representatives of the law in the city, and so, putting aside his personal feelings in the matter (for he was very fond of Cassio), he removes his lieutenant from

[1] Henry N. Hudson. *Shakespeare's Life, Art and Characters*, page 474, Vol. II.

office. And, having these high motives, he must have been more than a little annoyed at Desdemona's putting her plea on the ground of personal friendship. We may be sure that if Cassio could have gotten an interview with Othello, he would have acknowledged his offense against the official (Montano) and would have asked permission to explain his peculiar weakness as regards to strong drink.

Somewhere along the way the presence of Bianca in the play must be considered. She serves an important place in the plot for her participation in the handkerchief episode. Perhaps, also, her presence may have tended to throw suspicion away from Cassio and Desdemona. One can easily imagine the groundlings at the Globe saying coarsely, "Why should he be interested in the Governor's lady when he had a woman of his own?" Evidently she had followed Cassio from Venice. That he was ashamed of the relationship is shown by the fact that he did not wish Othello to see him in her company. She should not be permitted to detract from an estimate of Cassio's character.

Othello's description of his wife as one who "loves company,/ Is free of speech, sings, plays and dances well," gives us a picture of a girl with more than average enthusiasm. This would explain, in large part, her persistence in championing the cause of Cassio once she had undertaken the task. And the fact that Cassio had acted as go-between during their courtship would enter into the plan and make it seem a natural thing to do.

The hiding behind a petticoat scheme (for so it rather appears to be) had originated in the crooked mind of Iago. A certain reluctance on the part of Cassio about becoming a participant in the plan is indicated by his leaving Desdemona's presence abruptly and trying to avoid a meeting with Othello and Iago. Also, and perhaps much more important, Cassio may have been no little disturbed by Iago's suddenly ingratiating himself with Othello. He had stood between the two in rank and knew both of them thoroughly, and any close friendship between them would have been almost unthinkable to him. Something of this kind may have been in his mind when he said to Desdemona that he was "very ill at ease." With his hurried departure begins what is called the "temptation scene" as Iago says to Othello, "I like not that."

We must agree with M. R. Ridley when he says, "It would be idle to try to analyze the famous 'temptation scene,' (III-III); it must be read in its entirety and slowly, as we watch Iago moving slowly, almost stealthily forward step by step, testing each foothold before he moves to the next." [1] So there will be no attempt here at a full analysis of the scene. However, out of this scene two questions arise, questions which aim to probe the very foundations of Othello's character. These two questions are: (1) Was Othello gullible? (2) Was Othello jealous? But the two questions are so closely related that their answers must necessarily overlap and intermingle somewhat. A fairly conclusive answer to the question of gullibility can be found in the lines of the play itself, but the proof of jealousy is not so easily traced. A careful reading of the play finds Othello resisting the very thought of Desdemona's faithlessness from the beginning. Soon after Iago's "I like not that" Othello says, "There is some monster in his thought too hideous to be shown." He accuses Iago of having some horrible conceit shut up in his brain. Next he says, "She had eyes and chose me. No, Iago I'll see before I doubt." Again he says, "If she be false then heaven mocks itself. I'll not believe it." Even after he is half convinced, when he has said farewell to the plumed troops and the big wars, he exclaims, "Villain, be sure you prove my love a whore,/ Be sure of it; give me ocular proof." Then he adds, "If thou dost slander her to torture me,/ Never pray more."

There is no gullibility here. There is alertness, but there is no suspicion. When Othello says, "I think my wife be hon-

[1] *Shakespeare's Plays, A Commentary* by M. R. Ridley, page 161.

est and I think she is not," he has begun to doubt. But still he insists, "Give me a living reason she's disloyal."

It is Iago's pretended sensitiveness about his honesty, followed by the story of Cassio's dream, which is related as defiant proof of his honesty, that brings final conviction to Othello. When Othello says, "All my love thus do I blow to heaven" the climax of the play is reached. Then finally there comes that fatal, "O thou art wise!" and Othello has capitulated completely not so much to Iago's arguments and insinuations as to Iago's "honesty" and "wisdom."

Suddenly in the midst of the temptation scene Iago delivers himself of that speech which has become so well known even to people who are not serious students of Shakespeare: "Who steals my purse steals trash." This speech has long been regarded by scholars as a rare bit of philosophical wisdom which Shakespeare interpolated into the play and casually gave to Iago. No one, whose interpretation I recall, has seen it as an echo of Cassio's lament about the loss of his reputation. The psychopath has an uncanny way of catching an idea, we might even say pouncing upon an idea, of another person and elaborating it into such a scintillating version of the original that its origin can scarcely be traced. This seems the most likely interpretation of the speech when we accept Iago as a psychopath. Another possible explanation of the speech is this: may it not be that in the stillness of the night Iago's seldom-aroused conscience has told him that in stealing money from Roderigo, he has been stealing mere trash; but in robbing Michael Cassio of his good name, he has stolen something that has not enriched himself but has made Michael poor indeed? In either case the speech harks back to Cassio's lament about the loss of his reputation. Also, the two explanations might easily be tied together, the temporarily aroused conscience suggesting the eloquent, pompous elaboration of Cassio's comments in the psychopathic manner.

Aside from an appreciation of the beautiful poetry near

its close, the temptation scene is not one to which we return with any degree of enjoyment. It is so very harrowing. I can go again and again to Inverness Castle on the night of that terrifying storm when Duncan was murdered. I can stand at the foot of that stairway and watch once more that kindly man come staggering down the steps, reeling under the first impact of the weight of a guilty soul. I know that he will lash out at life. I know that he will lash out at his fellow men in a half-insane, desperate attempt to allay the sting of the scorpions with which his mind is filled. He will harbor the vain delusion that one more person removed from his path will enable him to sleep in spite of thunder. I know that he will go on from murder to murder until the undiscriminating will never be able to think of him as anything but a murderer. Yet for one brief moment I have glimpsed a beautiful soul so sensitive that it will never be able to bear the heavy burden of sin. But the sight of Iago's sadistic torture of the noble Othello is almost beyond human endurance.

And Iago? As has been said, cowardice is one of the distinguishing marks of the psychopath. That Iago was a coward is shown convincingly in his keeping himself safe behind the scenes while others carry out the details of his nefarious schemes. His cowardice played no small part in trapping him in the end. His final plans go astray. Cassio is only slightly hurt, and Roderigo lives long enough to reveal all of Iago's villainy.

Often when the abnormal human being who is commonly called a psychopathic personality is caught in the toils of his own wickedness, or less serious defections, he will blurt out the truth, and this confession often tells the entire story of his abnormal actions. Iago's statement about the daily beauty in the life of Cassio which showed up his own ugliness explains all his devilish villainy with its growing complexity and resultant tragedy. It was not hatred of Othello that incited his desire to "trap them all"; it was not suspicion of Othello and

Emilia; it was not the promotion of Cassio; it was not injured feelings of any description. It was Iago's deep-seated envy of the daily beauty in Michael Cassio's life that lay at the bottom of this great tragedy. In Cassio there was an inner light that is rarely seen in men, and Iago resented that inner grace with all the force of his being. It was a gnawing thing that he kept within his own breast, while outwardly he built for himself, for his own protection and for his own egotistical edification, that house of cards—his invincible "honesty," and this house of cards was only a cheap imitation of what he so stubbornly and reluctantly and secretly admired in Michael Cassio. Iago's last speech is: "Demand me nothing. What you know you know./ From this time forth I never will speak word." The psychopath never faces anything. When confronted with a difficult situation, large or small, he invariably crawls into an evasive shell. So Shakespeare's psychopath remains true to type to the very end.

Meanwhile "honest Iago" has become a "slave." The word is on every tongue. "Slave" in Shakespeare's time was used as a term of contempt.[1]

In Othello's last speech, made by permission of the officials who are about to take him captive, he speaks proudly of his services to the state. He requests his hearers to send a truthful account of him and his actions to the Senators at Venice. In characteristically poetic vein he goes on to speak of a time in Aleppo when he smote a turbaned Turk. Again his rich voice and measured accents compel the fascinated attention of his audience so that he is able to stab himself before they are aware of what he is about to do. So he goes out, poet to the last.

At the close of the play the punishment of Iago is left to the new Lord Governor of Cyprus, Michael Cassio.

In the Globe Theatre the part of Iago was played by a strapping young actor of twenty-eight, named John Lowin.

[1] See "slave" O.E.D.

Lowin had joined the Company the summer before and had played the part of Claudius in *Hamlet*. Cassio was played by Henry Condell[1] who had been with the Company since boyhood when he played the parts of young ladies. The previous summer when *Hamlet* was given he had played the part of Horatio. So the audience saw the Claudius-Iago actor given over to the tender mercies of the Horatio-Cassio actor, and as they left the theatre they may have been wondering what punishment would be metered out to him, or if that punishment would be severe enough.

And William Shakespeare, sitting in his study where most of his characters were born, would know that Iago's fate was already sealed. Would it be suicide, he would ask himself, or would there be a complete mental and physical collapse, which would separate him permanently from contacts with his fellow men? Or, could it be possible that Iago might still adjust himself to normal relations with his surroundings? At this last question he would shake his head and turn to another task.

This, then, briefly and from one point of view, is the story of Othello. It is a story of innocence and nobility and honor becoming the victim of the evil that can exist in an abnormal mind. It is a story as old as the recorded history of man. It is a story as new as the latest edition of today's newspaper. Yes, there are many, many stories on this old, old theme, but the one about the valiant Moor towers mightily above all the others in the magic charm of its telling.

[1] This is according to Baldwin's table, in *The Organization and Personnel of the Shakespearean Company*.

KING LEAR

Tʜᴇʀᴇ ɪs an introduction to *King Lear* that never has been written. Editors of the play include in their introductory matter discussions of the date of composition, the source material used by Shakespeare, and the history of the play on the stage. The commentators see the play as a bright jewel in the mosaic of literature that had been written up to the age of Elizabeth. The average student, however, has not the background of study nor, perhaps, the desire to go into a great deal of preliminary matter; so to him *King Lear* is seen only as a story of family life. It is as such that it will be dealt with in this study.

The story is laid in primitive Britain when that little island was still largely covered over with forests. Some "clearings" there must have been with towns and the beginnings of towns, but the greater part of the population centered in and around London. There were no feudal castles. King Lear had ruled over this almost mythical land for half a century. Living in a peaceful country in comparatively tranquil times Lear had had no opportunity to become a great king according to standards of later, more warlike times of ambitious conquest. But he was proud of being a king. During the long years of his reign there had been in his heart and mind the constant ideal of being a kingly person. He loved the lush meadows, the rippling streams and the shadowy forests that were his own possession, though he probably had not traversed their length and breadth to any extent. As the years passed he became an imperious king in the sense of demand-

ing certain standards without necessarily being overbearingly
dictatorial. He gave all his time to affairs of state. For long
years the thought never crossed his mind that he would not
always be King of Britain.

Then he passed his eightieth year. His towering strength,
though still mighty, was beginning to totter. There were
days when he was not able to leave his room. Then into his
chambers came his youngest daughter, the lovely Cordelia.
She ran her soft young hand over his brow and did many little things to make him comfortable, all the while speaking
words of encouragement and cheer in a voice that was soft,
gentle and low. She sat beside him and talked when he wished
conversation, keeping silent when she sensed that he preferred to rest. When he was well enough, they sat by the fire
and talked of many things. She found that she could make
him laugh heartily. He told her of the strivings that went on
at court, how one group would get into power and another
go out. He made it an entertaining story when he had never
seen the amusing side of the situation before. And once he
said, "They tell me I am everything, but I sometimes suspect"
—Wearily he left the sentence unfinished. They exchanged
stories, too, he recalling old tales he had known from boyhood and she repeating stories she had heard from the servants and from wayfarers, who had stopped at the palace. The
rain came down on the roof, the fire crackled on the hearth,
and they were loath to break the spell of the enchanted hour.

One day she brought her three little puppies. Their names
were Tray, Blanch, and Sweetheart. The dogs knew nothing
of royalty, and so they licked the King's face and chewed at
his bony hands, and the old man liked it. The eyes of the girl
and the man met in laughter at the tricks of the dogs. But by
this time the meeting of their eyes had begun to show affection and then undisguised love.

In the night when Cordelia was gone the old King lay on
his bed thinking, thinking, hearing again the low tones of the

beautiful voice and seeing again her youthful grace as she moved about the room. A great longing came over his tired spirit, a longing to spend the remainder of his days resting on her kind nursery. A plan began to take shape in his mind, and as he turned it over in his thoughts all the details of the plan began to fall into place. He could see no possibility of failure. He would divide his kingdom between his three daughters, giving the larger share to Cordelia with the understanding that he was to live with her. As the days passed and Cordelia spoke freely of her love for him, the old man began to cherish a dream that became more and more precious to him, a dream in which he saw Cordelia telling the people of the court of her love for her father. Yes, the sycophants would be told that he had three daughters who loved him. Poor man! He had lived so long in the public eye that he saw no impropriety or bad taste in such a procedure. He did not realize, or had forgotten, that often the most priceless things in life cannot fittingly be dragged into the limelight. So he continued to mature his program.

Then one day Cordelia finds herself in a courtroom of the palace presided over by an eagle-eyed old king who is her father but bears little resemblance to the kind father she had known in the sick room. He has a map before him and is telling the assembled lords and ladies of the court that it is his purpose to cast the cares of state from his failing strength and to place them on younger shoulders. He declares his intention of dividing his kingdom between his three daughters and, in return, he will ask each of them to tell the court how much she loves him. Cordelia knows that neither Goneril nor Regan loves their father, and she waits with her heart in her mouth. Goneril answers glibly with a ready declaration of her love for her father, and Regan follows with an even more extravagant statement. Cordelia realizes that she will be called upon next. She recoils from vying with her false-speaking sisters, and she resents the manner in which the question is put to her, her father asking her to make a stronger declaration of her love in order that she may receive a larger, more opulent portion than those of her sisters. It must be admitted that the manner in which Lear puts the question is quite tactless. This, no doubt, irritated Cordelia. Little excuse can be found for the old King's crudeness except, perhaps, that the court itself was lacking in the refinement that would have required a more discriminating handling of the delicate situation. This would suggest a refinement in Cordelia that was above her surroundings. Yet, later, we find Albany speaking of Lear as a "gracious aged man." [1]

True to herself Cordelia asks her heart, "What shall Cordelia do?" and the answer comes spontaneously, "I can only love and be silent." Then in answer to her father's pressing question she speaks that fatal word "Nothing." At first Lear cannot believe what he has heard and asks her to mend her speech a little. When he is finally convinced that she means to deny her love for him, he denounces her and banishes her from the kingdom. Cordelia's answer, it must be admitted, was a public affront to her father, the King. When Kent tries to intercede for her Lear says, "I loved her most and hoped to set my rest on her kind nursery."

This line, spoken to Kent, is the most important line in the play, although it has been sorely neglected by many scholars, many of whom find the division of the kingdom "incredible folly," or childish "play acting" when there is the sound reason, given by the King himself, that he wished only to spend his declining years with Cordelia, having her take care of him. What could be more natural or sensible except his impulsive stripping himself of everything after Cordelia had rejected his offer? But, it must be repeated, the whole play pivots on that one line "I had hoped to rest on her kind nursery." That Cordelia disappointed him by seem-

[1] Act IV, Scene II, line 41.

ing to repudiate him and their great love is one of the most
tragic things in Shakespeare. My imaginary, and perhaps
unusual (but I hope not too presumptuous), sketch of the
sick room scenes has been based on that statement by Lear. In
defense of my description, if it needs defense, I would ask:
Why would Lear be willing to divide the kingdom if he had
not had some previous experiences of having Cordelia care
for him in a sick room?

When Cordelia goes out with her final admonition to her
sisters to treat their father well, the two fall to discussing
their father's uncertain temper which they say has increased
with the years. During the conversation Regan makes the
statement that he has "ever but slenderly known himself."
One should not expect pearls of wisdom from Regan, but
her remark has been given more attention than it deserves.
It seems better to turn to Lear's own statement that "They
told me I was everything." The people of the Court had flat-
tered him and gave him nothing by which to measure himself.
So they cruelly left him to find out in his declining days that
he was not ague-proof.

Lear makes his greatest mistake when he divides the "more
opulent third" between the two older sisters. The division of
the kingdom into three parts had been given careful attention, and no one could question its reasonableness, but the
forcing (for it seems almost that) of the other third on Goneril and Regan was done in his terrible rage against Cordelia.
The mistake is founded, of course, on his belief that Goneril
and Regan also love him. And we may well believe that the
more opulent section lost its attractiveness to him when he
knew it could not be shared with Cordelia. Critics have been
very severe in their criticism of Lear up to this time. They see
nothing but foolhardiness and senility in the division of the
kingdom. A popular lecturer, whose talks on TV aroused a
keen interest in Shakespeare and, no doubt enriched the lives
of many people, made the statement that Lear was a "hollow

turnip." Whether the remark was intended to be facetious or not, it was no less than shocking to the serious student of Shakespeare not to mention the misapprehension it brought to the uninitiated. Surely William Shakespeare never would have dissipated his great talents by writing about hollow turnips. All of these critics admit, with too little clarification, that Lear had a great awakening toward the end of the play, but according to my reading Lear had a beautiful awakening before the play begins, an awakening to the beauty of the love that can exist between parent and child. And it was because of this belated, tender awakening that he made his original decision to divide the kingdom.

To be sure, anyone who can read can get some understanding of the meaning of *King Lear*. But if he has reached the time of life when he has a goodly sprinkling of gray hair, if he has grown children, if his experience has given him some understanding of Lear's comparison of a thankless child with the sharpness of a serpent's tooth, if he knows what it means to have given too much, if he has known the bitter tongue of a child who has said something equivalent to Regan's unspeakably cruel, "And in good time you gave it," if he knows what it means to be disappointed, even for a short space of time, in the one on whom he had counted most, if he has become aware that it is possible for a human being to be so direly in need of divine help and yet be so heavily weighted down with years that he doubts if heaven itself be old enough to understand—then he will begin to have some real comprehension of *King Lear*.

So Lear takes up his residence with Goneril, and the first time we are permitted to see him in his new surroundings, he comes in from a day of hunting, ravenously hungry and orders that his dinner be served promptly. Immediately we sense that all is not well, or there would be no need for the demand as he puts it.

Instead of a plentiful dinner served promptly his weary

old nerves are subjected to a shrewish tirade about the supposed misbehavior of his hundred knights whom he had specifically stated he would keep when he divided the more opulent part of the kingdom between Goneril and Regan. Some
scholars seem to sympathize with Goneril in spite of the fact
that we are permitted to hear her instructions to Oswald
to see to it that Lear's men are slighted and ignored by the
regular servants of the household. Also, her husband, Albany,
has no knowledge of disorderliness among Lear's men. In an
aside one might ask: Who would believe Goneril in prefer-
ence to Lear?

When Lear slowly realizes the meaning of what Goneril
is saying and trying to do he calls for his horses and then
curses her. Oh, how he curses her! Lear's great agony has
begun before he leaves the domain of Goneril, and at the
close of the curse we have that immortal line, "How sharper
than a serpent's tooth it is to have a thankless child."

While Lear and the Fool wait in the courtyard for their
horses the Fool keeps up running comments intended to cheer
and amuse the King, who answers absentmindedly because his
thoughts are elsewhere. Suddenly he says, "I did her wrong,"
and we know he is thinking of Cordelia. Make no mistake
about it, Lear's love for Cordelia runs through this play like
a bright thread, frequently hidden and again brilliantly dis-
played in all its great beauty. There in the courtyard, too,
Lear realizes what all the recent happenings are doing to his
mind. Scholars who like to trace the progress of Lear's insanity will probably find the first steps here in Lear's own
fear of going mad.

He finds his way to Regan's palace, believing that he still
has a daughter who will be loyal to him. His only attendants
are the Fool and a Gentleman, doubtless one of his train, but
Kent had been sent on before with letters to Gloucester and
will join them later. Failing to find Regan and her husband
at their own home, which they have fled to avoid receiving

him, Lear makes his weary way to Gloucester's Castle, where he finds Kent in the stocks and refuses to believe that Regan and Cornwall have placed him there. When Gloucester brings him the excuses that have been given him to deliver —that they are sick and weary and have travelled all night —Lear's shocked, pained, angry incredulity makes one of the saddest pages in the book. In his long speech we have our last glimpse of the imperious king of whom most of the older critics write, when he says, "The King would speak with Cornwall," but immediately he adds, the dear father would speak with his daughter. Then he makes excuses for the Duke and accepts the statement that he is not well. But recalling the picture of Kent in the stocks he again makes a demand that they come forth and hear him. His command, however, lacks something of the old imperiousness. In fact, that side of his character came to an end with the banishment of Kent in Act I, Scene I. True, there seems some of it in his demand that his dinner be served immediately but, examined more carefully, it is an expression of resentment at the lagging service he has been receiving. In the scene under discussion his angry demands and threats have a strong note of helplessness in them. He realizes that his heart is beating dangerously fast, and he cries to it to calm down.

When Regan and Cornwall make their appearance Lear begins to tell Regan how Goneril has struck at his heart with sharp-toothed unkindness, but when Regan tells him he does not know how to value Goneril's desert the old man says in bewilderment, "Say, how is that?" Regan continues to defend Goneril and even goes so far as to suggest that Lear ask her forgiveness. Almost stupidly he overlooks her blunt reference to his age and her suggestion that he should be ruled by others who know his state better than he himself does. In a mocking bit of acting he pictures himself begging that Goneril grant him raiment, bed and food because he is old, and age is unnecessary. Regan rebukes him for his "unsightly

tricks," and orders him to return to Goneril. The conversation between father and daughter goes on, and the reader
finds it difficult to comprehend how the old man blindly
continues to trust Regan, overlooking her insulting refer-
ences to his age and her defense of her sister. The only possible explanation must be that he is stubbornly or stupidly
clinging to his thought that she loves him as Cordelia did.

When Goneril arrives Lear is confused and hurt to find
Regan taking her by the hand. The conversation continues
with both daughters taunting their father with weakness and
dotage and carrying on with him a bickering dispute about
the number of followers they will permit him—the former
King. When Regan has beaten the number down to twenty-
five and says, "To no more will I give place," the old man
stares at her blankly for a moment and then says slowly,
"I gave you all," and Regan answers with incredible cruelty,
"And in good time you gave it." One might search throughout all the plays of Shakespeare and not find a more hard-
hearted remark than this—"In good time you gave it." They
continue with their questioning of his need for twenty-five
or even five, and then Regan says, "Why need one?" Lear
begins to philosophize about need, saying that even beggars
may have more than they need. As he tries to elaborate his
thought his own great need overwhelms him, and he cries to
heaven to give him patience which is his true need. This
speech about the needs of mankind ending in his strong statement of his own great need for patience seems to belie the
impression many scholars have that Lear has lived his eighty
years without thinking very seriously about anything. Their
conclusions seem to be based on the fact that he had taken
too little time to understand his daughters and on Regan's
statement that he had ever but slenderly known himself. Just
what Regan's observation means is not too clear, but one is
foolish to expect pearls of wisdom from Regan. Many students are all too willing to accept the word of the Gonerils

and Regans and Iagos of Shakespeare. In this play, too, scholars seem to confuse Shakespeare's Lear with the tinsel king in the Chronicle Play from which parts of Shakespeare's story were taken. George Kittredge says of these two kings: "He," the Lear of the Chronicle Play, "is distinctly senile. He has all the futilities of old age with none of its dignity. *But in Shakespeare Lear becomes colossal.*" Patience is the one thing he needs, the King repeats. Then the once imperious King begs the gods to see him here a poor old man as full of grief as age and wretched in both. He warns the gods that if it be they who have stirred up his daughters' hearts against him they must not fool him so much that he will take it tamely. He begs them to touch him with noble anger and not permit tears to stain his manly cheeks. He turns his wrath again upon his daughters whom he sees now as unnatural hags. He warns them that he will have such revenges on both of them that all the world shall—he stops, unable to finish the sentence or to think what he expects of the world in connection with his daughters. His next broken sentence is so moving that it reminds one of a helpless, frightened child clenching his fists and trying to tell some domineering grownup what he will do in retaliation. He is going to do such things, Lear says—he does not know yet, but they will be the terrors of the earth. Again like a child he is on the verge of tears, and the daughters stand by expecting him to break into weeping, but he defies them and declares that he will not weep. He has full cause for weeping, he tells them, but his heart may break into a hundred thousand pieces before he will weep. Then he turns to the Fool and says, "O, Fool, I shall go mad," as he rushes out of the house. And the sympathetic reader feels an impulse to close the book and read no more of the pitiless treatment of this kindly old man.

Once he is safely out of the house the two hypocritical daughters pretend that they would have received the old man gladly without his followers. They put the blame for his tragic exit on his own folly and smugly conclude that he must take the results of his own dotage.

So they turn him out into the night with its cold and rain —the white-haired old man who less than a month ago was the proud King of Britain. And now in place of his regal power and obsequious subjects he has only a faithful fool to keep his weary feet from letting him down into the mud and mire. Old age has descended on him with cruel suddenness.

Kent and the Gentleman have made their exit with the King but have become separated from him. They meet and Kent gives the Gentleman a commission to Cordelia, who has learned of a brewing war between Cornwall and Albany and has crossed the channel with an army to protect her father. Kent then joins Lear and the Fool and remains with him to the end.

Any attempt to describe the storm on the heath would be as great a piece of literary affrontery as one could commit. If, however, he is alert to Shakespeare's sense of words and could grasp all their connotations and implications, his single word "pitiless" would serve as an adequate description. It was a pitiless storm. Or, Kent's description might be quoted in which he says that the wrathful skies terrify the very wanderers of the dark, animals who are protected by nature against the elements by heavy coats of fur and the like have crawled into caves for safety. Kent adds that he never remembers to have heard such bursts of horrid thunder, such groans of roaring winds, or to have seen such sheets of fire. It is not in man's nature, he says, to bear such afflictions nor such fear. Or, for a hint of the storm's terror, we might turn to a later scene in the play and ponder Cordelia's statement that her enemy's dog, though it had bit her, might have lain by her fire that night. But any explanation of this scene must carry Lear's own words in order to convey his reactions to the storm and its effect on him.

Before continuing this part of the study, I should like to

mention a company of Shakespearean players from Europe, travelling in America, who presented this scene with a brilliant, dazzling spotlight on Lear who was clothed in a gorgeous red velvet robe, and this unimpressive personality stood on a not too stable elevation reciting the majestic lines of the immortal King Lear. Surely Shakespeare intended this scene to be played on a darkened stage with Lear's white hair, blanched face and imploring hands outlined against a pitchy blackness and with these white features eerily illuminated occasionally by flashes of lightning.

Lear shouts at the storm, bidding its winds blow and rage until they have cracked their cheeks. He cries to the cataracts of rain to spout until they have drenched the steeples and drowned the cocks on their summits. He sees the lightning as a sulfureous fire which precedes the thunderbolts that split the sturdy oaks that have stood for so many centuries, and he defies the lightning to singe his white head. He shouts at the all-shaking thunder and commands it to strike at the round earth and lay it flat. He charges the thunder to destroy all the seeds of life that make ungrateful man. The Fool advises him to go back and beg his daughters' blessing, but as usual Lear disregards him and shouts to the storm to rumble its bellyful, the lightning to spit fire and the rain to continue to spout. They, the elements, may fulfill their purpose, and he would not try to hinder them, he says, because they are not his daughters, and he cannot accuse them of unkindness since he never gave them kingdom or called them his children, and they owe him no submission. So they have every right to express their horrible pleasures. Then his train of thought changes, and he sees himself as a slave of the elements, their slave, a poor, infirm, weak, and despised old man. And yet these elements are servile underlings because they have joined their powers with those of his two pernicious daughters against a head so old and white as his. He is overcome with these thoughts and can say only, "O, O, 'tis foul!"

The Fool has rightfully been praised for his loyalty to King Lear, but he is Shakespeare's poorest psychologist in that he continuously harps on the pernicious daughters and on Lear's folly in giving them the kingdom.

Ignoring the Fool, Lear is trying to get control of his feelings and says, "No, I will be a pattern of all patience. I will say nothing." At this point Kent joins them. He gives his description of the storm already mentioned, ending by saying that it is not in man's nature to endure such fear as this storm has engendered.

But Lear has begun to have his own interpretation of the storm. Disregarding the presence of Kent, he says it is the gods who are making this dreadful pother over their heads, and these gods are dreadful summoners from the Court of Heaven who have been sent to charge sinners to stand up and confess their sins. He names some of these sinners: the perjurer, the murderer with the bloody hand, the adulterer, and the impostor who practices his rascality against his fellow men. Lear imagines himself surrounded by these people to whom he addresses himself. He tells them to tremble for their individual crimes, to hide their bloody hands and cry mercy to these dreadful summoners, the heaven-sent gods who have come to ask an accounting from each individual. He visualizes, or feels, these offenders crowding around him. Then he thinks his own time has come to answer, and, looking up at the lowering heavens, he says, with simplicity and sincerity, "I am a man more sinned against than sinning." This is his accounting of his life to the eternal gods. This is Lear's finest hour.

This sentence is one of the many lines of Shakespeare that have been mouthed by the ignorant and illiterate to whose ears it has filtered down through unknown channels. It has been repeated by weaklings who scarcely comprehend its meaning but like its sound, it has been whined by prostitutes to hide the ugliness of their abhorrent way of life. In short, the sentence has been used by the shallowest and most debased of mankind until it has lost much of its significance and all of its touching beauty; so we must go back to the heath with its flashes of fire and bursts of horrid thunder and try to recapture something of its original meaning. And this man who has taken his place among the sinners his conscience tells him of and has given his own honest reply to the demands of the almighty gods is the same man who, less than a month ago, was king of a beautiful land. For many years he had loved that land, but he had been willing to give it all to his daughters asking only their love and the little care that an old man needs as he crawls toward death.

Kent has entered, still in disguise, and tells Lear of a hovel near by that will give him some protection from the storm. Lear comes out of his abstraction and realizes that the sinners whom he has been admonishing really are not present. Dazed and bewildered he says to Kent that his wits are beginning to turn. He accepts the offer of the straw bed in the hovel and philosophizes about how strange it is that our necessities can make vile things precious. Even though his wits may be turning he has become a philosopher.

Inside the hovel they meet with Edgar. This necessitates a recognition of the secondary plot of the play. Most critics are of the opinion that the Gloucester story adds greatly to the interest of the play as a whole. They regard it as a kind of reflection in the water that enhances the beauty of a mountain or other object, as a striking duplication of the Lear story. Be that as it may, this secondary plot adds little or nothing to the study of Lear's character and so will not be considered here. It would complicate instead of simplifying or clarifying the character study.

But Lear is not yet insane. Far from it. In a conversation

he has with Kent before the hovel, he tells Kent that he probably thinks this is a great storm because it has drenched them to the skin, but when a greater illness is present a lesser one is scarcely felt. He goes on to say that the tempest in his mind takes from his senses all feeling except what beats in his thoughts. Then he comes to the thing that has been uppermost in his mind and exclaims against filial ingratitude. First his mind turns to punishment of his daughters, but he is having a struggle to keep from weeping and sets his will against such a weak display of feeling. He becomes more specific and exclaims against his daughters' shutting him out in such a night as this. He speaks their names reproachfully and then adds, "Your old kind father whose frank heart gave all!" This takes us back to the beginning of the play and to the comments of the students who see that division of the kingdom only a display of ego or stupidity, or a piece of childish folly. Obviously they have come to their conclusions from reading the first scenes and have not added to that view of Lear these serious, intense scenes. If they had waited to get the whole picture, they would have been convinced that, even though his wits are beginning to turn, this old man is not stupid. We have just seen him standing up before a heavenly judge with all mankind, as he thinks, admitting that he is not without sin but declaring that others have greatly sinned against him, and we know he is speaking the truth when he tells his daughters he was their kind old father whose frank heart gave all. But he has learned, as Hamlet knew, the danger of thinking too intently on events, and he shudders at the thought that he will go mad if he continues to follow this course of thought.

Then we have that pathetically beautiful speech in which he addresses himself to all the poor naked wretches of the world and wonders how their lack of homes, their nakedness and their hunger can defend them against such a storm as this. He expresses a moving regret that he has taken too little thought of these unfortunates. He addresses himself to the people on the pompous side of life and bids them expose themselves to the conditions in which the poorest wretches live so that they may rid themselves of many superfluities that surround them. And then, he concludes, things will be more equally proportioned, and the heavens may seem more just. His wits may be turning, but King Lear is thinking more deeply, and seemingly more rationally, than he ever has done before. This tendency to philosophize cannot be a sudden development. His daughter Regan and the fuzzy-minded critics[1] notwithstanding, he must have had some definite bent in that direction before the play begins.

Much has been written about Lear's great awakening but little that is specific. I find that during the storm Lear has learned two things: First, that man is accountable to a Higher Power for his conduct here and, second, that man is responsible to a great extent for the well-being of the unfortunates of his own little world. To have learned these two fundamentals of life after his eightieth year after he had been deceived and shielded and lied to does, indeed, constitute a great awakening.

On seeing Edgar disguised as a madman, Lear asks if giving all to his daughters has brought him to this plight, and we see the dangerous trend of his thoughts. Kent tells him that Edgar has no daughters, and Lear declares that nothing could have brought him to this condition except his unkind daughters, and Kent is a traitor to say otherwise. He tells Edgar he would be better in his grave than exposed to such a storm. A man not supplied with clothing from the worm, the beast, the sheep is only a forked animal, he adds. He begins to tear off his own clothes, and at this point, it is agreed, his wits have completely turned.

Gloucester joins them and after telling Lear that Goneril and Regan have commanded him (Gloucester) to bar his

---

[1] Of course I am not calling all the critics fuzzy-minded. Heaven forbid!

doors against Lear and leave him at the mercy of the storm, he suggests taking the four of them, Lear, Kent, Edgar and the Fool to a farmhouse near his castle where there are both fire and food. There Lear enacts that pathetic trial scene wherein he arraigns his two daughters. The pungent line in the scene comes when he speaks of Cordelia's dogs, Tray, Blanch, and Sweetheart, and thinks that even they have turned against him. Kent gets him to lie down when Gloucester returns and tells them the news that there is a plot against the King's life. He has a litter ready and urges Kent and the Fool to take the King to Dover where Cordelia has landed with an army to protect her father in the threatened war between the two sons-in-law. Arriving at Dover and being told that Cordelia is close by, Lear refuses to see her because, as Kent tells the story, his own unkindness that stripped her of his benediction stings his mind so venomously that burning shame detains him from Cordelia.

But the King is still "mad" and is found wandering about the fields dressed in weeds and talking wildly. His mind seems clear on one thing, however. The people of the English court were not men of their word. They told him he was everything, and he was not even ague-proof. Back and forth his wandering thoughts go, coming to rest always on his rejection by his older daughters. When the attendants, whom Cordelia has sent to find him, appear, he tells them he needs a surgeon because he is cut to the brains. He is taken to Cordelia who has a physician ready to minister to him. His frayed nerves are quieted by nourishing food, and his mental derangement is cured by kind nature's sweet restorer, sleep. When he awakens to the strains of soft music, we are permitted to witness the tender reconciliation of the two who never should have been separated. The doctor asks Cordelia to take her father "in," and the two walk a little distance together. Thus we are permitted to compare two mental pictures, one of an imperious old King standing in rich

royal robes, towering above his people, pointing a threaten-
ing finger at the noble Kent and banishing him from the
kingdom, and now the same man in ill-fitting garments,
shambling along beside his strong, young daughter, looking
the picture of happiness and the embodiment of humility.
The humility is not a servile one—not Lear who had been so
proud of being every inch a king—but a beautiful, serene
humility that is the afterglow from having found a personal
contact with the Infinite and of holding out his hand, though
belatedly, to the needy of all mankind.

The best brief summary, or analysis, of Lear's madness is
given by George L. Kittredge.[1] It is as follows: "Lear's
madness has no place in the old story; it is Shakespeare's own
invention. Eminent alienists have diagnosed it as senile de-
mentia. His mind was failing, they contend, at the beginning
of the play. To the Elizabethans, however, irascibility was
not insanity. Nothing can be clearer than that Shakespeare
intended Lear's madness to be simply an attack of feverous
delirium brought on by exposure to the storm and superin-
duced by the terrible strain to which his emotions had been
subjected. The physician actually cures him. Even the dreadful events that follow do not overthrow his restored reason,
for when he enters with the murdered Cordelia in his arms
he is not mad. At the moment of death when his powers fail
utterly, so that he cannot recognize his nearest friends, it is
not madness but dissolution."

Lear and Cordelia are being taken to prison. Cordelia suggests seeing her sisters with the thought of interceding with
them, but Lear shudders at the thought. He pictures the life
they may live in prison. They will sing like birds and laugh
and tell old tales. They will talk of the court and of who's in
and who's out. This is reminiscent of the picture presented
at the beginning of this sketch when the two were presented

[1] In the Introduction to the play in his edition of the Complete Works.

together in the sick room. Lear wishes only to be with Cordelia, even though it be in prison.

But an order has gone out for the execution of Lear and Cordelia. Part of the plan miscarries, and only Cordelia is hanged. Lear comes in carrying her slender body. He will not believe she is dead when a dog and a horse can be alive. He tries the tests of a feather and a mirror to see if she is breathing, but the feather does not stir, and the mirror remains clear. Cordelia is dead, and "there is nothing left remarkable beneath the visiting moon." [1] Kent, with the wisdom of the ages, knows that there is nothing more in life for Lear, that life from now on would be only torture for him. The restoration of the hundred knights or the return to the land that he had loved would mean nothing to him now. Cordelia is dead, and the light of his life has gone out. Lear faints, and death comes easily to him.

And if we should look for the fatal flaw in the character of Lear which brought about his downfall, it seems to me at this reading that it was a fatal acquiescence, not necessarily a weak acquiescence, but a too friendly one which permitted him to accept the court life as it was, including the flattery that was heaped upon him, thus shutting him off from all practical experiences of normal life and any proper evaluation of himself. (This takes us back to Regan's—or Shakespeare's—statement that he had but slenderly known himself.)

Hamlet had staggering problems thrust upon him at the very outset of life. Lear lived more than eighty years with little or no knowledge of treachery and certainly no conception of ingratitude and what it can do to a man. Along with the delayed experiences that came to him in the last few weeks of his life was a revelation of love. The marvel of the story is that he learned so quickly, once he found the hollowness of his elder daughters' protestations, and realized that he

---

[1] *Antony and Cleopatra.*

had done a great wrong to Cordelia. When he was turned out into the pitiless storm this old man, who but a few weeks ago had but slenderly known himself, stands up before the thundering gods and gives them a brief and true characterization of himself. And when the great rage was killed in him, he saw himself only as a foolish, fond old man ready to ask forgiveness from his rejected daughter. The tragedy of Lear is that his experience of life came too late.

Read with serious attention Lear is a heart-rending story, as, indeed, are all the great tragedies. Dante, we often have been told—and Horatio Bridges puts it this way—"was the man who had been in hell; and Dante never quite got out again, because they could always see it in his face. But the man Shakespeare did not reveal to his fellows what he had seen and known. His triumph was that after Lear he still could laugh. . . . With Lear's Gethsemene embodying itself in his mind, he sat in taverns and drank wine with mortal men."